Dina Matar is lecturer in Arab Media and International Political Communication at the Centre for Film and Media Studies, the School of Oriental and African Studies. She was formerly a foreign correspondent and editor covering the Middle East, Europe and Africa. She is also a co-editor of the *Middle East Journal of Culture and Communication.*

What It Means
to be Palestinian

Stories of Palestinian Peoplehood

Dina Matar

I.B. TAURIS
LONDON · NEW YORK

Published in 2011 by I.B.Tauris & Co Ltd
6 Salem Road, London W2 4BU
175 Fifth Avenue, New York NY 10010
www.ibtauris.com

Distributed in the United States and Canada
Exclusively by Palgrave Macmillan
175 Fifth Avenue, New York NY 10010

ISBN: 978 1 84885 457 4 (hb)
      978 1 84885 363 8 (pb)

A full CIP record for this book is available from the British Library
A full CIP record is available from the Library of Congress

Library of Congress Catalog Card Number: available

Printed and bound in Great Britain by TJ International Ltd, Padstow,
Cornwall

Mixed Sources
Product group from well-managed
forests and other controlled sources
www.fsc.org Cert no. SGS-COC-2482
© 1996 Forest Stewardship Council
FSC

For Henry

CONTENTS

ILLUSTRATIONS

PREFACE

How do you write a book on Palestine and the Palestinians when the very act of writing about, giving voice to, or representing the Palestinians is beset by two larger, inter-related problems: first that Palestinian history tends to be viewed solely in relation to Israeli history or narrative; and second that the story of the Palestinians, as ordinary human beings subjected to violent forms of power, remains a largely hidden one.

This book is a small effort amongst many others to address this problem. It sets out to tell a personal history of the Palestinians, in their own words, to provide a more human-ist understanding of what it means to be Palestinian in the twenty-first century. The memories and stories this book tells show that 'what it means to be Palestinian' cannot be reduced to a question of identity alone, often talked about as a politi-cal, national, collective or resistant identity that has been con-structed, as the Israeli narrative often suggests, as a category of being in relationship to a significant 'Other', Israel. Rather, as the stories included in this narrative suggest, 'what it means to be Palestinian' is about lived experiences and conditions 'of being' which change and shift as a result of evolving circum-stances and conditions. In different and complex ways, these circumstances are linked to the *Nakba*, the catastrophe of 1948, when the state of Israel was created and the Palestinians were denied their land and, most importantly, their commonality with other human beings.

Today, there are over ten million Palestinians, half of whom live within what was known as Historic Palestine, in the Gaza Strip, the West Bank and inside Israel, while the rest are scattered across the Middle East and beyond. West Bankers and Gazans continue to live under occupation and stringent movement restrictions imposed by Israel; those in East Jerusalem are 'permanent residents', but not citizens of Israel; the rest are citizens of the self-proclaimed state of the Jewish people with negligible political influence.

The Palestinians outside these areas exist in conditions ranging from utter misery, as in the refugee camps in Lebanon, to varying degrees of comfort in assorted Arab countries, Europe, the Americas and other regions of the world. These Palestinians 'of the diaspora' (*al-shatat*) possess a variety of passports, *laissez-passers* and refugee documents. Their conditions vary, but most are united by two facts: that their parents or grandparents were obliged to leave their homes and that they are barred from living in any part of their ancestral homeland. In telling remembered lived experiences in individuals' own voices, this book seeks to ascribe agency to the Palestinians, not as helpless victims of forces beyond their control, as they have often been portrayed, but as *actors* at the centre of critical phases of their modern history.

This book speaks to all Palestinians, but it does not speak *for* them. I dedicate it to those Palestinians who so generously gave me their time, invited me to their homes and offered me food, drink and places to stay, sometimes in refugee camps in Beirut, Damascus, Amman, Bethlehem, Nazareth, Haifa, Jaffa, Nablus and Jerusalem. In particular, I want to mention those young Palestinians whose stories I did not include, but who helped me understand. So I express my thanks to Dyala and Bisan in Yarmouk Camp who took me round tirelessly to meet friends and relatives, to Fadi

Dabaja and Zahra in Burj al-Barajneh Camp in Beirut, to Juliette, Jita, their parents Therese and Suheil in Nazareth, to my cousin Samira in London and my cousin Nabil Matar in the United States, and my family in Canada and the occupied West Bank.

I was inspired by many scholars and writers, but two of them stand out for helping me think beyond the bounds of convention: Rosemary Sayigh, for her thought-provoking and humanist ethnographic accounts of the refugee camps in Lebanon, and Lila Abu-Lughod for the fresh anthropological approaches in her various studies of Egypt and which draw attention to our common humanity, and the need to give space to individual voices.

I write this book in memory of my father, Henry Matar, who wanted to do this project with me, but died well before it saw the light of day, and of Edward Said, whom I never met, but whose voice so vividly articulated the aspirations of the oppressed and marginalized. His intellectual contribution went beyond Palestine, because his was a universal, conciliatory and humanist message that resonated with any audience interested in justice and human dignity as the most compelling forms of truth.

This book would not have been possible without the brilliant and meticulous translation and intellectual support of Dr Atef Alshaer, my colleague and friend at the School of Oriental and African Studies, nor without the moral and unfailing support of my husband, John, and my son Henry. I also thank my dear colleague and friend Melanie Saint-Cyr for taking time to go through the manuscript, point out inconsistencies and turn it into a better narrative. There are many others to thank, but I express particular gratitude to my friends and colleagues Dr Lina Khatib and Dr Tarik Sabry, my co-editors at the *Middle East Journal of Culture and Communication*, to Isabelle Humphries, for her support and help with names and missing information, to Juliette Touma and her family in Nazareth, to

Khalid Ali in Damascus, and to my cousin Nabil for his enthusiasm and continued support. I also thank Rich Wiles and Tanya Habjouqa, whose photographs bring this book to life. Finally, I cannot thank Philippa Brewster at I.B.Tauris enough for her enthusiasm and belief in this book.

PROLOGUE

What separates us from the 'characters' about whom we write is not knowledge, either subjective or objective, but their experience of time in the story we are telling. This separation allows us, the storytellers, the power of knowing the whole. Yet, equally, this separation renders us powerless; we cannot control our characters.... We are obliged to follow them, and this following is through and across time, which they are living and which we oversee. The time, and therefore the story, belongs to them. Yet the meaning of the story, what makes it worthy of being told, is what we can see and what inspires us because we are beyond this time. (John Berger)

This book is a narrative of narratives: a collection of personal stories, remembered feelings and reconstructed experiences by different Palestinians whose lives have been changed and shaped by history. I relate these stories and convey them within a chronology that corresponds to certain phases in the history of the Palestinian national struggle. I bring them together to form a composite, though incomplete, 'biography' of Palestine – as a landscape and as a people. These 'stories of peoplehood' provide intimate views of history,[1] yet differ from conventional history in that they are not always told in a chronological order.

The historical phases that frame the stories begin with the 1936 revolt against British rule in Palestine and end with the Oslo peace agreement between Israel and the Palestine Liberation Organization, signed in 1993, transforming the nature and form of the Palestinian national struggle. Since the phases within this period tend to stretch further in some definitions than others, and in any case overlap, the years marking their beginning and end – indicated by the chapter titles and the historical background with which the chapter opens – by no means indicate clear-cut boundaries. The chronological frames contrast with the discursive and lyrical stories within each chapter to show that telling and remembering are continuous processes of provisional and partial reconstruction of personal and collective history that struggle with and against a still-contested present.

Narratives are always situated: they have an audience and a teller. They are partial, and their telling is intentional.[2] The stories I tell are not different. Although they reveal a great deal about the personal complex and diverse experiences of Palestinians in the past, before and after the *Nakba* ('catastrophe') of 1948, they must be understood in the present context, within which they were told and narrated, and read as sites of struggle between at least two overlapping contests, the internal struggle between popular and official nationalist views and the international struggle between Palestinian and Israeli views of the history of the conflict.[3] As such, they can be seen as attempts to adapt to rapidly changing landscapes and continuing violence, irrespective of whether this violence is experienced by the narrators themselves or by others in a similar situation. This is the violence of uprooting and destruction: the violence visited on Palestinians by their enemies, the violence that Palestinians visit on others and the violence Palestinians have wreaked on each other. This is also the violence that is talked of – in the manner of the Western mainstream media – as part of a repeated 'cycle of violence in an intractable conflict' that has brought the Palestinians a great deal of world attention and heightened their self-awareness, while exacerbating their sense of being a community set apart from others.[4]

Throughout the three years I spent researching and writing this book, Palestinians – particularly in the occupied territories and Gaza – were locked in a process of 'terror, counter-terror, violence, counter-violence',[5] very like the process Frantz Fanon described in his writings about the anti-colonial struggle in Algeria. In those three years, Palestinians in the Gaza Strip, the West Bank and East Jerusalem lived under conditions of siege, continually squeezed into or out of changing and diminishing spaces, enduring an Israeli blockade of towns, crippling economic measures, land confiscations and military attacks on civilian areas. Palestinians in Israel, though citizens of Israel, have continued to endure socio-political discrimination and other restrictions.[6] In exile, the fate of millions of refugees banished from their homes remains as unclear as ever.

Recording the stories

This book is based on in-depth interviews and conversations with a diverse group of Palestinians, male and female, old and young, rich and poor, in the Israeli-occupied territories, Jordan, Lebanon, Syria and Israel in 2007 and 2008. I conducted the interviews in Arabic, apart from a couple in English. I had some people in mind to approach before I started the research. Once I was in the field, I was led from person to person by Palestinians who wanted me to speak to individuals that they knew to have witnessed, or been involved in significant events in Palestinian history.

I was struck by the intense need to tell and record personal narratives. 'Why don't you want to hear my story?' was a question I often heard after long, intense and thought-provoking days listening to stories and remembered experiences. This desire to tell and be heard (I am not suggesting this is peculiar to Palestinians) suggests that talking about and remembering the self does not stem from a previously defined, static identity with specific features, or from a need to restore an original identity; rather, it is a continuous process of 're-membering, of putting together moment by moment and of provisional and partial reconstruction'[7] of the past in the present.

Emerging from these narratives was the sense that, though the narrators themselves might agree on the actual and constitutive elements of a shared history and ways of life, and recognize the defining effects of these on their remembered experiences, what they cherish and hold on to are their own feelings, experiences and interpretations of these experiences. The individuals in this book speak in a personal, subjective way, though together they give a credible account of critical events during their lifetime. Bearing all this in mind, I do not claim that my narrative is representative of all Palestinians, that it covers all events in Palestine since 1936, that it encompasses every experience of those events or that it incorporates all the diverse political, ideological and religious orientations of Palestinians.[8]

I write this book as part of an intellectual tradition, continued by various scholars in different disciplines, aiming to capture the complexities of Palestinian experiences through personal stories. I draw on the methods of oral history research and the concerns of popular memory scholarship, both of which celebrate and give voice to the subaltern and the marginalized. My narrative, however, differs from recent academic oral history writing in both style and presentation. I wanted to write in a form accessible to a wider audience, not just the scholarly and the elite.[9] It also differs in its historical scope (I do not limit the research to one period or one event), in its inclusion of both marginalized and non-marginalized Palestinians (some scholars, for example, have focused on the refugees in Lebanon)[10] and in the geographical areas it covers: Jordan, Lebanon, Syria, the occupied territories and Israel.

I let people tell their stories with minimal editorial inter-
vention, keeping as close as possible to the form and structure in which these memories, stories and experiences of the
past were evoked, even though almost all were translated from
Arabic. I was wary of generalizations that could make the subjects – the 'others' we research – seem at once more coherent,
self-contained and different from 'us' than they might actually
be.[11] Therefore, I do not present these accounts as abstracted
facts about the past, or as clusters of sociological and cultural
interpretive frameworks, as is common in anthropological and
social science monographs, but as remembered personal narratives that in their simplicity, partiality and complexity provide a dense and intimate ethnographic story of what it means
to be Palestinian in the twenty-first century.

Selection and construction

Putting together these accounts was not a question of mere
narrative technique, but a complex process of selection and
construction in which I, as researcher, author and narrator,
was implicated from the beginning, starting with the selection
of people I interviewed and ending in the choice of those
stories I make public here. In total, I interviewed and recorded
the stories of 80 male and female Palestinians of diverse ages,
socio-economic backgrounds and religious or ideological
orientation. Some were more forthcoming than others; some
were more evocative and lyrical; some more precise and
concise; some more emotional; some more restrained; some
more secular; some more religious.

I talked to 'public' or prominent Palestinians who have been
and continue to be politically active, ordinary Palestinians who
were nevertheless involved in the armed struggle in its various
forms, and others who were not active at all. I spoke to refugees in camps in Beirut, Damascus, Amman and Bethlehem,
to town and city dwellers, to Palestinians who remained inside

Israel in 1948, and to Palestinians inside the occupied territories. I limited the geographical area to Jordan, Lebanon, Syria, the occupied territories and Israel because all of these were – and continue to be – deeply involved in the key events and political developments of the Palestinian–Israeli conflict since 1948. I include narratives by Gazans interviewed in places outside Gaza because of Israeli restrictions on entry to and blockade of the strip imposed since 2007. I use real names in almost all the accounts apart from a couple of cases where I decided to use pseudonyms to ensure the narrators' anonymity and safety.[12]

I did not categorize the narrators by gender, age, socioeconomic, ideological or religious background because these categories would have abstracted and reified divisions that become self-explanatory in the stories themselves. I did not think imposing these categories was necessary, given that the chapters are arranged chronologically with the intention of providing a remembered biography of Palestine as a landscape and as a people. My main challenge in selecting and putting together this narrative was to decide whose stories to tell.

In taking these decisions, I was conscious of being deeply implicated in deciding whose version of reality counts as history and which version counts as the truth. Despite my training as a journalist and a social scientist, this challenge made me acknowledge that remembered experiences and truth do not necessarily overlap, that there can be multiple truths about events without diminishing either the significance of remembering or the importance of finding out what 'really' happened, as Nadje al-Ali also argued in her book on Iraqi women.[13] In the end, I was guided in my selection by those remembered experiences and stories that fitted well within the chronological structure, by those that served as valid documents bearing a particular truth-value to experienced events, by those that were more complete and coherent than others, and by those that excited and moved me. Where and when possible, I tried to verify statements, dates and names of places by corroborating information from other documents and recorded histories. Although, all the personal narratives in this collection of life stories are translations, they aim to interpret faithfully Palestinian colloquial language,[14] experiences, senses of self and senses of others. I tried to make my selection of narratives for each chapter as representative as I could, it was impossible to include all the stories I was told, but I wanted to recognize and show the complex and elusive nature of Palestinian identity. These stories integrate public and private realities, and through them we can apprehend the extraordinary variety – and experiences – of individuals called Palestinian.

In telling their stories, the narrators move across time and space, marking out the trajectory of a continuing *Nakba*. There was, as Lena Jayyusi notes about her own interviews with *Nakba* survivors, an urgent need to repeat tales that are similar, but different, that shape and make explicit the unique and continuing character of the catastrophe, as each 'new tale is an echo within the echo, focusing and conjuring up the collective predicament through the individual one, while ramifying the significances and symbolic meanings of the individual experience through the collective.'[15]

What follow are not life stories or narratives in the conventional sense, but fragmented compositions of experience and existence, self-consciously staged testimonials that occasionally contain, along with the individual's experience, the assertiveness and stridency of the collective Palestinian nationalist stance and rhetoric. Some of these stories are undoubtedly punctuated by what is clearly an uncomfortable silencing about some events or occasions of lack of action, a reluctance to make public the Palestinians' own failures, complicity, culpability or collaboration, as well as the violence that Palestinians have visited on others or wreaked on each other and the sense of shame, if not guilt, that this can also bring. Though the stories are partial and incomplete, each speaks to what Edward Said

called the 'much more fugitive, but ultimately quite beauti-
fully representative and subtle, sense of identity. It speaks in
languages not yet fully formed, in settings not completely
constituted, like the shy glance of a child holding her father's
knee while she curiously and tentatively examines the stranger
who photographs her.'[16]

Popular memory

This book aims to complement, rather than subvert, the
top-down approaches prevalent in most modern histories of
Palestine and adds to the burgeoning oral history and popular
memory research on the Palestinian people pioneered by the
important ethnographic work of Rosemary Sayigh and that
of Nafez Nazzal in the 1970s.[17] Oral history is a method of
gathering historical information related to specific events,
experiences, memories and ways of life and includes various
forms of in-depth interviews, such as life stories, personal
narratives and accounts of specific historical events.[18] Oral
history (also used by journalists, including the late Studds
Terkel)[19] offers an intimate and humanistic window on the
past by allowing people to tell their stories and interpretations
of events in their own words. Oral history theory and practice
has undergone four paradigm shifts related primarily to the
growing significance of personal testimony in such areas
as political and legal practices; the inter-disciplinarity of
approaches to interviewing and interpretation of memory
and the proliferation of studies in the 1980s concerned with
the relationship between memory and history.[20] The popular
memory approach complements oral history, but is more
interpretive in that it does not take the explanatory value of
personal narrative at face value.[21] As Louisa Passerine writes,
'the guiding principle could be that all autobiographical
memory is true: it is up to the interpreter to discover in which
sense, where, for which purpose.'[22] What matters are the

ways in which people produce the past through a dynamic
engagement with the present, a production that involves a
range of modes of telling – what we call discourses, official
and popular, dominant and oppositional, individual and
collective. The final analysis is inherently relational:

> It has to take in the dominant historical representations in the
> public field as well as attempts to amplify or generalize subordi-
> nated or private experiences. Like all struggles it must [needs
> to] have two sides. Private memories cannot, in concrete studies,
> be readily unscrambled from the effects of dominant historical
> discourses. It is often these that supply the very terms by which
> a private history is thought through .... Similarly the public dis-
> courses live off the primary recording of events in the course of
> everyday transactions and take over the practical knowledge of
> historical agents.[23]

Memory, Pierre Nora writes, is always a phenomenon of the

> present, a bond tying us to the eternal present; history is a
> representation of the past. Memory, being a phenomenon of
> emotion and magic, accommodates only those facts that suit
> it. ... History, being an intellectual, nonreligious activity, calls for
> analysis and critical discourse. Memory situates remembrance
> in a sacred context. History ferrets it out; it turns whatever it
> touches into prose.... Memory is an absolute, while history is
> always relative.[24]

Although some aspects of Nora's definition of memory
tell us much about its construction and selectiveness, his argument that history is universal whereas memory is essential is
problematic, and the distinctions 'hyperbolic'.[25] In fact, recent
scholarship on history as a cultural construction tends to per-
ceive memory as a collective project that is crucial to the con-
solidation or construction of group, community or national
identities, and a site of hegemonic struggle between dominant
and subordinate discourses and histories.[26]

There is nothing simple about memory,[27] and perhaps
(though not uniquely) for Palestinians 'there is no forgetting

memory, no way of overlooking it.'[28] Memory is almost always mediated. On the one hand, it assumes a past outside the person's subjectivity that is recalled in the present and, on the other, it requires a narrator who is equipped with conventional cultural filters (generational distance, age and gender, class and political affiliations) and on whose authority the truth of the past can be revealed. Memory, as a discourse about the past and of the present suggests that its meanings are not fixed in stone, but are malleable, shifting and open to interpretations and judgements. Memory can be a tool in the hands of people in power, or an ally for those who are dominated and those whose voices are not heard. The work of memory, then, must address itself not only to questions of what happened, but also to how we know things, whose voices we hear and where silences persist. Memory can help create nations, but it can also tear nations apart, because it is often mobilized to support nationalist projects and discourses, for projects of state-building and projects of power. Memory can call into question the status quo and 'can slip through the holes in the wall' of dominant discourses. It is in this sense that memory can speak truth to power.[29]

Talking to Palestinians, sharing their anxieties about the present and their nostalgia for an idealized past, watching television news with families – often in utter silence, seeing the enormity of another Israeli incursion into Gaza – discussing the most recent Palestinian exploits, internal rifts and shifts in positions and alliances, talking everyday politics in cafés, on the streets and in taxis and buses, and drinking many cups of black coffee and tall glasses of sweet mint tea, I became aware that personal memories, however subjective they are, can carry both general and more particular meaningful truths. I also became aware that there is no single Palestinian memory, but memories that cut across many types of memory – social, historical, cultural, individual, collective and sensual.[30] What ultimately emerges from these stories is that Palestinian memory is, at its heart, political.

What is 'it' we ask?: and what to make of answers

How is Palestine as a landscape and a people imagined and remembered by the Palestinians to whom I spoke and whose stories I tell? Which events do they remember most and want to talk about? Which events are preserved in their subjective selves and which (parts of) events are actively suppressed? Which parts remain hidden in fragments of individual memory, only to re-emerge in moments of crisis or reflection? What do these events, refracted through personal memories, mean for the present and for the collective Palestinian political and moral claim to justice and redress? These are key questions for scholars of memory, and these were the types of question that I asked in order to explore what was experienced and what was remembered. The stories told here do not provide all the answers, but fragments of answers that seemed to be significant for the narrators themselves.

In pulling together these narratives, it became clear to me that if I were to remain true to the remembered experiences as they were told me, I could not collate them as a grand narrative or as a standard anthropological or social science monograph. I was reluctant to use a form of writing and interpreting in which the 'Palestinian' has often been treated as a mere 'object' of academic study, rather than a human subject, or as the invisible component, though the central one, of what has entered public and media discourses under the generic name of the Palestinian Problem, the Palestinian Cause or the Palestinian Question.

Edward Said, though he himself used some of these generic terms, evocatively talks about this, and the production of the Palestinian as a commodity:

> Producing ourselves much as *masabih*, lamps, tapestries, baskets, embroideries, mother-of-pearl trinkets are produced. We turn ourselves into objects not for sale, but for scrutiny. People ask us, as if looking into an exhibit case. 'What is it you Palestinians want?' as if we can put our demands into a single neat phrase.[31]

Emerging from these personal stories was a deep desire to humanize the Palestinian story and to tell of remembered experiences that meant something to the narrator, however subjective these memories might be. Also emerging from the stories was the persistent theme that Palestinian sense of displacement was not the result of one specific event, but an ongoing process, continuing into the present. Indeed, what existed in the past – the 'there' of memory – is still there. But it is because it is irredeemable and inaccessible that it has 'acquired the complex, impersonal texture of an ancient wall: you can neither have it, nor penetrate it. Yet curiously, this aspect of the past can be re-inscribed in the present. It does affect our sense of where and how each of us is now.'[32]

The 'there' of Palestinian memory keeps coming back to a key date: 1948. At the beginning of that year, the Arabs of Palestine constituted an absolute majority of its inhabitants – defining Palestine as the area within the borders of the British Mandate between the Mediterranean Sea and the Jordan River – and they owned nearly 90 per cent of the privately owned land. Within a few months, more than half of the country's Arab majority, between 850,000 and 1 million people, according to most estimates, were expelled or forced to flee from the area, most of which became the state of Israel. About 150,000 Palestinians remained within Israel, which by then controlled 78 per cent of the territory of former mandatory Palestine.

In a few weeks in the spring of 1948, Jaffa and Haifa, the cities with the largest Arab population in Palestine and the most dynamic centres of economic and cultural life in the British Mandate, were seized by Zionist militias, led by the Haganah forces, which later formed the core of the Israeli army. Most of the Arab population of these cities was dispersed and their property taken over. Virtually all Palestinians were expelled from the coastal plain between Jaffa and Haifa, and from along the road between Tel Aviv and Jerusalem. Jewish control was also established over the western half of Jerusalem, forcing thousands of Palestinians to flee to the eastern part and beyond. The combined forces of the Palestinian fighters of Jaysh al-Jihad al-Muqaddas ('Holy War Army'), the Arab forces of the Jaysh al-Inqadh ('Arab Liberation Army') and other Palestinian irregulars could not repel the attackers and did not pose an effective, co-ordinated challenge to the onslaught.[33] The reasons for this are well documented elsewhere.[34]

Zionism, founded as a secular political ideology by Theodor Herzl (1860–1904), had not originally seen Palestine as the only possible location for a Jewish homeland;[35] there were thought to be other options too. However, the fall of the Ottoman Empire, the mandate of the League of Nations that placed some Ottoman territories under British rule, the close relations between leading Zionists and members of the British government, and other international and local factors combined to make Mandate Palestine the most realistic object of Zionist aims.[36] Waves of Jewish immigration (*aliyah*) had begun in the 1880s, fluctuating over subsequent decades until numbers soared following the Nazi Holocaust with the influx of large numbers of European refugees.

On 1 April 1948, the Haganah put into action the Zionist master plan for gaining and maintaining control of Palestine. Plan Dalet,[37] the basis of the assault, spelled out that any armed force in the villages targeted should be erased and their populations expelled beyond the borders of the state. In those villages that did not mount any resistance, Zionist troops would take control and detain all politically suspect individuals. Villagers deemed suitably compliant would be appointed to work under a Jewish superior to manage the political and administrative affairs of the village following the occupation.[38]

More than 531 Palestinian villages were destroyed and 11 urban areas were emptied of their inhabitants in the resulting war of 1948, 'a clear-cut case of an ethnic cleansing operation, regarded under international law today as a crime against humanity'.[39] Palestinian refugees, forced to leave their homes, became the most visible Palestinian constituency, the community that embodied the experiences of Palestinian rupture and dispossession – they were, and remain, the *mankoubeen* ('the catastrophed').[40] Those who stayed behind became known by the contested label of Israeli-Arabs.[41] They were, and remain to this day, nominal citizens of the new Israeli state, which subjected them to a system of military rule by a government that confiscated much of their land and kept them under close surveillance for 18 years. They were invisible for most of the two decades after the *Nakba*, except for when members of divided families would send heart-breaking greetings and news on radio stations. In their own language, they were the *mansiyyin* ('the forgotten'). The remainder of the Palestinian population, in the West Bank, whether refugees from other parts of Palestine or native to the area, were put under the repressive regime of Jordan's Hashemite rulers, while those in the Gaza Strip were placed under the uncaring Egyptian administration. Both areas were seized by Israel in the 1967 Arab–Israeli War and placed under military occupation.

In a short period, 'Palestinian society was violently extracted from its moorings in space, fractured along multiple axes, expelled and undone.'[42] 'The Palestinians do not exist,' claimed the new masters, excluding and silencing them *tout court* from their own unfolding historical narrative, a narrative that twinned the birth of the state of Israel on what was previously Palestinian land with the re-birth of the Jewish people following their persecution in Europe and subjugation to Nazi genocide. This narrative has since described the Palestinians' fate in convenient and general terms, reducing it to a question of desperate refugees who were seen, at best, as a humanitarian case, deserving only the support of UN agencies – support that they often experienced as demeaning.[43]

Rashid Khalidi writes that revisionist history, of the sort that has emerged (in Israel, in particular) in recent years, requires as a foil an established authoritative master narrative that is fundamentally flawed in some way.[44] In this sense, the excavation of Israeli governmental and institutional archives in the 1980s by a number of Israeli historians and social scientists – Avi Shlaim, Benny Morris, Ilan Pappé and others – served to argue against and seriously disturb the Zionist nationalist myth behind the establishment of the state of Israel. This myth has informed and shaped Israeli accounts of that country's history and served as the backbone of the received version of the history of the conflict as it is perceived in the West.

The modern Zionist movement originally imagined that Eretz Israel ('the land of Israel') was empty. 'A land without a people, for a people without a land' was the slogan invented by the Zionist Israel Zangwill,[45] allowing Zionism to come fully into its own 'by actively destroying as many Arab traces as it could'.[46] Although they broke boundaries within Israeli official historiography, through the examination of Israeli archival material, the mainstream new historians' movement did not begin to address or create a history that placed Palestinians as human subjects or agents in their own history. In fact, Ilan Pappé writes that this new trend in history writing could have resulted in a political breakthrough in the battle over memory in Palestine, but 'we, the new historians, never contributed significantly to the struggle against the *Nakba* denial as we sidestepped the question of ethnic cleansing and ... focused on details.'[47] The sense of responsibility goes further, he says: 'In the case of Palestine and Israel, history is no longer a pastime, a career, or a profession; it is a commitment to involvement for the sake of oneself, as much as that of others.'[48]

Organizing the book

For readers not familiar with Palestinian history, each narrative chapter begins with the background to the period, written in the more conventional form of a factual historical account.

This sets the scene and alerts the reader to the possibility of reading the book in a particular way and suggests connections to subsequent chapters.

The narratives, personal stories, experiences and reflections of 6 to 8 Palestinians in each chapter are organized by a historical period, which may determine how they are read and interpreted. The chronological structure is meant to draw attention to links in the remembered stories and personal experiences, not to argue for a particular uni-linear sequence of causality.

Chapter One is bracketed by the year 1936, the beginning of the three-year Arab revolt in Mandate Palestine, and 1948, the year of the *Nakba*. Relying mainly on personal life stories, I decided that the late 1930s was as far back as I could go, given that the oldest Palestinians I talked to were in their late seventies. Central to this chapter are stories by diverse Palestinians in different places about their experiences leading up to the catastrophe and of the catastrophe itself. The stories reflect the diversity of experiences, while validating historical accounts that the *Nakba* itself was a result of a coordinated plan meant to raise fear and anxiety and force the inhabitants from their homes.

Chapter Two explores various memories of living through the *Nakba*, inside and outside the camps, in Arab countries and in Israel itself. The period, loosely bracketed by the events of 1948 and 1964, is often referred to as the 'epoch of silence' or the 'lost years', reflecting how the Arab Palestinian community ceased to exist as a social and political entity. There was utter silence as urban life in the coastal cities disappeared and entire villages and city neighbourhoods were erased; about half of Historic Palestine's Arab inhabitants became refugees. The experience of exile would overshadow everything else for the *Nakba* generation.

Chapter Three examines people's experiences of resistance and struggle as part of the Palestinian revolutionary movement. The years between 1964 and 1970 marked the height of the national struggle both in exile and inside Israel as guerrilla movements, including Fatah, took over as the political and symbolic representatives of the Palestinians.

Chapter Four covers the period from 1970, when civil war broke out in Jordan, to 1982, the year of the Israeli invasion of Lebanon, which ended with the departure of the Palestine Liberation Organization (PLO) from that country. It was in 1974 that Yasser Arafat, chairman of the PLO but in military uniform, addressed the United Nations. This chapter includes stories by Palestinians in the occupied territories and inside Israel.

Chapter Five includes memories and experiences of the first Palestinian *intifada*, which began in 1987. By 1991 the uprising had been violently crushed by Israel and this, along with other regional factors, set the scene for the signing of the Oslo Accords in 1993.

This book has no formal discursive conclusion. A conclusion would have given closure and provided the reader with my own interpretation of these stories, as reflecting diverse aspects of Palestinian identity[49] which would have distracted attention from what they are about, remembered lived experiences of Palestinian lives in diverse spaces. Instead, I end with an epilogue that brings the history to the present. Unlike other chapters, I start with a few quotes that speak to the present. The epilogue keeps the story open and invites others to write similar histories of the recent or not-too-distant past.

Notes

1. Roger Smith (2003) *Stories of Peoplehood: The Politics and Morals of Political Membership*, Cambridge: Cambridge University Press.
2. Lila Abu-Lughod (1993/2008) *Writing Women's Worlds: Bedouin Stories*, Berkeley: University of California Press, p. 16.
3. Ted Swedenburg (2003) *Memories of Revolt: The 1936–1939 Rebellion and the Palestinian National Past*, Fayetteville: University of Arkansas Press, p. xxix.

4. The *Nakba* has made Palestinians much more aware of being Arab – their Arabness or Arab identity – while paradoxically driving a wedge between them and the rest of the Arab world.

5. Frantz Fanon (1963) *The Wretched of the Earth*, trans. Constance Farrington, New York: Grove Press.

6. Israel's right-wing government was debating a draft bill that would make it a criminal offence for Israeli citizens to mark the *Nakba*, according to a *Financial Times* report on 26 May 2009.

7. Nicola King (2000) *Memory, Narrative, Identity: Remembering the Self*, Edinburgh: Edinburgh University Press, p. 175.

8. The latest unofficial statistics show that there are about 10 million Palestinians worldwide.

9. It is worth mentioning the many books by Studs Terkel, recording Americans' memories of the Depression and of the two world wars, and Ronald Fraser's *Blood of Spain* in which he uses oral histories to put together a history of the Spanish Civil War.

10. See for example Ahmad Sa'di and Lila Abu-Lughod (2007) *Nakba: Palestine, 1948, and the Claims of Memory*, New York: Columbia University Press; Laleh Khalili (2007) *Heroes and Martyrs of Palestine: The Politics of National Commemoration*, Cambridge: Cambridge University Press; Swedenburg (2003) *Memories of Revolt*; John Collins (2004) *Occupied by Memory*, New York: New York University Press; and Susan Slymovics (1998) *The Object of Memory: Arab and Jew Narrate the Palestinian Village*, Philadelphia: University of Pennsylvania Press.

11. Abu-Lughod (1993/2008) *Writing Women's Worlds*, p. 7.

12. Some narrators wanted to be known simply by *Abu* or *Um*. *Abu* means 'father of' and *Um* means 'mother of'. Someone called Um Abbas would be a mother whose eldest son was called Abbas.

13. Nadje al-Ali (2007) *Iraqi Women: Untold Stories from 1948 to the Present*. London: Zed Books.

14. Palestinians speak Arabic, of course, but they have certain idioms and turns of speech peculiar to themselves and their place of origin.

15. Lena Jayyusi (2007) 'Iterability, cumulativity, and presence: the relational figures of Palestinian memory' in Sa'di and Abu-Lughod, *Nakba: Palestine, 1948*.

16. Said (1986/1993), *After the Last Sky*, London: Vintage Books.

17. Rosemary Sayigh (1979/2007) *The Palestinians: from Peasants to Revolutionaries*, London: Zed Books; Nafez Nazzal (1978) *The*

Palestinian Exodus from the Galilee, 1948, Beirut: Institute for Palestine Studies.

18. Nadje al-Ali (2007) *Iraqi Women*.
19. For example, Studs Terkel (1984) *The Good War* and (1970/1986) *Hard Times: An Oral History of the Great Depression*, New York: The New Press. Ronald Fraser (1979) *Blood of Spain: An Oral History of the Spanish Civil War*, New York, Pantheon Books.
20. See Robert Perks and Alistair Thomson (eds) (1998) *The Oral History Reader* London: Routledge for a detailed survey of the theoretical and critical developments in oral history research and its uses.
21. Key texts in this field include Passerine (1989 Popular Memory Group (1982) and Swedenburg (2003). The interdisciplinary study of memory has exploded in recent years because of growing interest in the ways wars, genocides, national liberation struggles and other violent periods are remembered.
22. Louisa Passerine (1989) 'Women's personal narratives' in Personal Narratives Group (ed.) *Interpreting Women's Lives: Feminist Theory and Personal Narratives*, Bloomington: Indiana University Press, p. 197.
23. Popular Memory Group (1982) 'Popular memory: theory, politics, method' in Richard Johnson, Gregor McLennon, Bill Swartz and David Sutton (eds) *Making Histories*, Minneapolis: University of Minnesota Press, p. 211.
24. Pierre Nora (1996) *Realms of Memory, Volume I: Conflicts and Divisions*, trans. Arthur Goldhammer, New York: Columbia University Press, p. 3.
25. Laleh Khalili (2007) *Heroes and Martyrs of Palestine*, p. 4.
26. Relevant work in the field of popular memory and the national past includes Anderson (1983/1991) *Imagined Communities: Reflections on the Origin and Spread of Nationalism*. London: Verso and Popular Memory Group (1982) 'Popular memory'.
27. John Collins (2004) *Occupied by Memory*, p. 10.
28. Edward Said (1986) *After the Last Sky*, p. 12.
29. I draw here on the theoretical and thematic points produced in the collective volume *Nakba: Palestine, 1948, and the Claims of Memory* edited by Ahmad Sa'di and Lila Abu-Lughod, in which the contributors outline the historical emergence of Palestinian collective memory, the challenges it faces and the moral and political implications of its erasure. This refers to the 'right of return', an internationally recognized right under UN Resolution 194 of 11 December 1948. This resolution stipulated that Palestinian

refugees should be permitted to return to the homes from which they were expelled.

30. This comes across in the ways in which smell and other senses can evoke memories.

31. Said (1986) *After the Last Sky*, p. 33.

32. Ibid., pp. 149–50.

33. Ghanem (2001) *The Palestinian-Arab Minority in Israel, 1948–2000: A Political Study*, New York: State University of New York Press, p. 15; Sayigh, *Palestinians: From Peasants to Revolutionaries*, pp. 77–81.

34. See, for example, Rashid Khalidi (2006) *The Iron Cage*, Oxford: Oneworld Publications.

35. Avi Shlaim (2000) *The Iron Wall: Israel and the Arab World*, London: Penguin, pp. 2–5.

36. Shlaim (2000) *The Iron Wall*, pp. 5–10.

37. Ilan Pappé (2006) *The Ethnic Cleansing of Palestine*, Oxford: Oneworld Publication, 'Plan Dalet', pp. xii, 2, 28, 40.

38. Walid Khalidi (1988) 'Plan Dalet: master plan for the conquest of Palestine', *Journal of Palestine Studies*, 18/1 (Autumn 1988), pp. 3–70, at p. 29.

39. Pappé (2006) *The Ethnic Cleansing of Palestine*, p. xiii.

40. I quote Joseph Masad from a talk he gave at the University of East London on 15 May 2008.

41. Palestinians use a variety of names for their community interchangeably – 'Palestinians inside Israel', '1948 Palestinians' or 'Arab citizens/sector/community' in Israel.

42. Lena Jayyusi (2007) 'Iterability, cumulativity, and presence' in Sa'di and Abu-Lughod (eds) *Nakba: Palestine, 1948*, p. 108.

43. See Julie Peteet (2005) *Landscape of Hope and Despair*, Philadelphia: Pennsylvania University Press; and Ilana Feldman (2008) *Governing Gaza: Bureaucracy, Authority and the Work of Rule, 1917–1967*, Durham, NC: Duke University Press.

44. Rashid Khalidi (2006) *The Iron Cage*, p. xxxii.

45. Karl Sabbagh (2006) *Palestine: A Personal History*, London: Atlantic Books, p. 6.

46. Edward Said (1986) *After the Last Sky*, p. 103.

47. Pappé (2006) *The Ethnic Cleansing of Palestine*, pp. xiv–xv.

48. Ibid., p. 119.

49. Abu-Lughod (1993/2008) *Writing Women's Worlds*, p. xxxi.

CHAPTER ONE

On the Road to *Nakba:* Palestine as a Landscape and a People, 1936–48

To be sure, no single Palestinian can be said to feel what most other Palestinians feel: ours has been too various and scattered a fate for that sort of correspondence. But there is no doubt that we do in fact form a community, if at heart a community built on suffering and exile. (Edward Said)

The decade from 1939 to 1949 marked a low point in the history of the Palestinians and their efforts to achieve their national objectives of independence and statehood. In 1939, *al-Thawra al-Kubra* ('the Great Revolt'), in protest against British colonial rule and the increasing Zionist threat, was violently crushed. The revolt was the most significant anti-colonial insurgency in the Arab East in the interwar period. It began with a six-month strike in April 1936, sparking brutal reprisals by the British rulers and leading to the declaration of a state of emergency.[1] Thousands of Palestinians from every stratum of society were mobilized, and significant numbers of peasants were drawn into the national movement. This marked the transformation of the *fallah* ('peasant') from an individual identified with the land into a symbolic representative of the cultural and historical continuity of the Palestinian people.[2]

Opposition to British rule and the Zionist threat had begun in 1929, when violence swept through Palestine. Following a minor incident over prayer arrangements near the Wailing Wall in Jerusalem, 300 Jews and a similar number of Palestinians were killed.[3] It was at around this time that 'Izz al-Din al-Qassam, the Syrian-born revolutionary leader and Muslim preacher, settled in Haifa, drawing followers from the northern districts where the influence of Jerusalem, the seat of political power, was traditionally weak. Qassam was killed[4] in the first encounter with British police in 1935, but surviving members of his organization continued to serve as a model and a catalyst for the widespread rebellion that unfolded in April 1936. By the mid-1930s, there were other signs reflecting the emergence of new forms of political activism. In fact, the first mass-based party, *al-Istiqlal* ('Independence'), was formally founded in 1932, as an outgrowth of pan-Arab groupings and ideologies that had long existed in Palestine and surrounding areas. It opposed British rule and was critical of traditional approaches to conducting politics, particularly by the *'ayan* ('notables'). Though short-lived – the party floundered in 1934 – *al-Istiqlal* was one of the few Palestinian parties with a clear ideology, broad membership and national support rather than a regional, local or family base. The political mobilization in the 1930s took place against a backdrop of increasing Jewish immigration and militarization, growing social dislocation and urbanization, which, along with other factors, eventually led to full-scale war.

The *Nakba*

The 1947–8 Arab–Israeli War marked the end of a lengthy chapter in the conflict over the possession of Palestine. The roots of this conflict lay in the emergence in the late nineteenth century of the European-based Zionist movement, dedicated to establishing a Jewish national homeland on the land of Historic Palestine.[5] Indeed, the *Nakba* ('catastrophe') that the Palestinians experienced as a result of the war and the creation of the state of Israel was the result of a vision set out starkly by Theodor Herzl, the founder of the Zionist movement, in his diaries in 1895.

Herzl wrote: 'We shall try to spirit the penniless population across the border by procuring employment for it in the transit countries, while denying it employment in our country.... Both the process of expropriation and removal of the poor must be carried out discreetly and circumspectly.'[6] Even as Herzl penned this down small numbers of Jews had already begun migrating to Palestine from Russia and Yemen for religious reasons, but it was the influx of politically motivated waves of immigration from eastern Europe in 1903 that stirred the first rumblings of discontent among Palestinian peasants opposed to the loss of land and jobs.[7] Concern over Jewish migration grew as signs of the Zionist policies of 'transfer'[8] began to emerge, particularly after Britain declared support for the establishment of a Jewish 'national home' in Palestine, spelt out clearly in the Balfour Declaration of November 1917.

By 1947, Britain could no longer control the Jewish community nor prevent armed conflict with the Palestinians. Responding to the impasse, the UN passed Resolution 181 in November that year, ending the British Mandate and supporting the partition of Palestine into two independent states: one Jewish and one Arab, each community occupying just under half of the territory. Although Jews by then constituted about a third of the population, the proposed Jewish state was to cover

56 per cent of the territory and would have only a slight majority of 499,000 Jews versus 438,000 Palestinians. The Arab state
was to occupy 43 per cent of the country and would include
818,000 Palestinians and fewer than 10,000 Jews.[9] The plan was
welcomed by the Zionists, but the Palestinian leaders rejected
it, refusing to sign away the right to sovereignty over any part
of the country. Confrontation between the two sides was inevitable, eventually drawing in the newly independent neighbouring Arab states, whose armies were poorly prepared.

The 1948 war unfolded in several stages, beginning with
local skirmishes and ending with the defeat of Arab contin-
gents from Egypt, Jordan, Lebanon, Iraq and Syria. In the process of establishing a Jewish state in 1948, Israel depopulated
and subsequently destroyed 531 villages across Palestine.[10]
Between 850,000 and 1 million Palestinians found themselves
in exile, outside the boundaries of the new state, and between
a fifth and a quarter of the 150,000–160,000 Palestinians left in
Israel became 'internally displaced' – prevented from returning to their homes, even with Israeli identity cards.[11] These
refugees, referred to as the 'present absentees', felt the full
brunt of Israeli policies and remain the most vulnerable of the
already marginalized Palestinian community in Israel.

The claims of memory

What do Palestinians remember of the years leading up to the
Nakba, or of the event itself? Which aspects of their lives remain
alive in their minds and how are popular memories of key
events re-figured and re-constructed over time, particularly in
the context of the continuing struggle for Palestinian national
rights?

In my interviews with diverse Palestinians in different
places, those old enough to have lived through the 1936–9
revolt and the decade leading up to the *Nakba* spoke about this
period in vague terms, referring to protagonists in the third

person.[12] Almost none of the people I interviewed chose to talk of the interwar years; but almost all, irrespective of who they were and where they ended up, had a personal story to tell about the focal date of 1948 and insisted on telling it. A similar structure of telling, in which personal stories converge on and intermesh with the collective (nationalist) Palestinian narrative of dispossession and loss, comes across in a similar corpus of work about the 1948 events, as it does in the burgeoning oral history scholarship concerned with memories of the *Nakba* itself.[13]

In talking about lives and experiences before 1948, the theme of rootedness – or an identification with particular spaces – comes up again and again, as does the theme of 'Palestine as Paradise' and that of the formerly proud family house, in the village, city or Bedouin encampment, left behind or wrecked. The same themes emerge in much of Palestinian literature and films. Indeed, over the years, Palestinian folk culture, conveyed by songs, ballads, poetry,[14] film and narrative, have formed around three motifs: praise and memory of the lost paradise from which Palestinians were expelled, lamentation of the present and depiction of the imagined return.[15] These have become the foundations for some of the most durable collective memories that have shaped Palestinian popular and nationalist discourses for more than six decades.

Place, as Sa'di and Abu-Lughod[16] note, has an extraordinary charge for Palestinians, not simply a site for memory, but as a symbol of all that has been lost and as a site of longing to which return is barred. This is true of many people, but the obsession with place and longing for the land seems especially characteristic of Palestinian memory because the *Nakba* was above all an exodus, a mass movement of people. It was also a collective experience that is remembered as a violent dismembering,[17] a violent uprooting that words cannot express and mourning cannot console, the memory of which came to haunt the inner history of the Palestinian people.[18]

In my interviews, it became clear that Palestinian memory is conditioned by present situations. Hence there is a romanticizing tendency to speak of an ideal existence before Palestinian society and ways of life were dismembered. 'We lived in Paradise' is a remark so often heard from older Palestinians – from those in refugee camps, in particular. Rosemary Sayigh has remarked on this 'sentimentality' in her monumental work on Palestinian refugees in Lebanon. 'It is true,' she wrote, 'that these dispossessed peasants have recalled their homes in Palestine from a present so bleak that their poverty and class oppression there tend to be blurred. But there is truth in their view of peasant life as good, for, in spite of poverty... village and clan solidarity formed a warm, strong, stable environment for the individual, a sense of rootedness and belonging.'[19]

I begin with a short account of my father's life in Jerusalem in the late 1930s, ending with his departure into exile in 1948. Though his leaving was voluntary, it was clearly a result of the events that led to the *Nakba*, the catastrophe. Henry Matar's short account of his experience as a teacher in the Old City of Jerusalem is the only story that was given to me in writing. He died before I could jog his memory further. The account is neither detailed nor overtly personal, but it conveys an image of a normal life cut off abruptly, but that continued nevertheless in exile. I wanted to start with a story of life in Jerusalem because the city always had immense political and religious significance for Palestinians and other Arabs, as well as for Jews.

During Ottoman rule, it was the capital of the *sanjak* ('district') of southern Palestine that included the sub-districts of Jaffa, Hebron, Gaza and Beersheba, together with 37 villages and the home territory of five Bedouin tribes. All these units reported directly to Istanbul.[20] During the British Mandate, Jerusalem was the locus of political power and the seat of the *a'yan* ('notables') who controlled high politics at the time, though other cities, such as Jaffa, Haifa, Nablus and Hebron[21] were also important for culture and trade. Jerusalem had some of the best schools in Palestine, and its newspapers, clubs and political leaders had an impact throughout Palestine, even before the British Mandate boundaries were established after the First World War. This was partly a function of the city's religious importance and partly because the city was the focus of the interests and designs of foreign powers.[22]

I follow my father's story with that of Sa'id Barghouti, later a member of the Palestine Liberation Organization and latterly an established writer and publisher in Damascus. He talks evocatively of his life in a village near Safad and then of his journey into exile, recounting with some detail his feelings as a young boy having to leave his home without his mother, while reflecting on his lack of awareness of what was really taking place. He eloquently sums up what a homeland means in a short sentence – 'A homeland has no borders' – evoking the sense of entrapment and siege that many Palestinians experienced after 1948.

The next four narratives are those of refugees in Beirut, Damascus, Bethlehem and Nazareth. All reminisce about peasant and Bedouin life in pre-*Nakba* Palestine, some in more detail than others, and all evoke a sense of loss, rupture and surprise at the suddenness of events. Salah Salah, who later became a leading member of the Palestinian resistance group, the Popular Front for the Liberation of Palestine, describes in a few words the conflict of identifications. 'It is like peeling off my skin,' he says of the time when he was encouraged to become a communist. Um Thabet, whom I interviewed in Yarmouk Camp, is perhaps the most articulate in conveying a picture of Palestine as a landscape and as a people, whereas Um Salah conveys the incessant feeling of fear and danger she experiences every day in the occupied territories. For her, life is a continuing *Nakba*. Abu 'Arab's story is the narrative of an internally displaced refugee who lives in Nazareth and can see but never lived in his home town, again conveying the sense of a continuing *Nakba* under Israeli rule.

The last story is an edited account of an interview with Shafik al-Hout, the former Palestine Liberation Organization representative in Beirut, who passed away in Beirut on 2 August 2009, well after I met him. In his story, he describes the beginning of grassroots Palestinian politics in Jaffa and his experiences as an exile now. It is fitting to end the chapter with a story from Jaffa, dubbed the Bride of the Sea, and the last Palestinian city to be occupied, on 13 May 1948, two days before the end of the Mandate. Jaffa was the largest city in Historic Palestine during the years of the British Mandate, with a population of more than 80,000 Palestinians. Another 40,000 people lived in the towns and villages in its immediate vicinity. By the 1930s, Jaffa was exporting many thousands of crates of citrus fruit to the rest of the world, providing jobs for the people of the city while linking them to the major commercial centres of the Mediterranean coast and the European continent.

While Jerusalem was the locus of political power, Jaffa was the cultural capital of Palestine. It housed the offices of leading newspapers – notably the dailies *Filastin* and *al-Difa'* – as well as ornate cinemas and prestigious clubs, such as the Orthodox Club and the Islamic Club, which have themselves become historic sites testifying to the city's cultural importance. In the Second World War, the British Mandate authorities moved the headquarters of the Near East Radio station to Jaffa, the broadcasting studios becoming a cultural centre in the city from 1941 to 1948.

When is politics? Henry Matar's story[23]

I did not think much about politics when I went to Jerusalem. Teaching students at the elementary stage took up most of my time and energy, and I had little time to think of anything else, though I did have time to make friends with fellow teachers from Jerusalem. They invited me to their homes, opening the doors to the Old City of Jerusalem and Islamic practices and ways of life in ways I, the son of devout Christian parents, would not have been able to experience on my own.[24] I spent the evenings of Ramadan, the Muslim fasting month, with them after breaking the fast at a café in the Old City listening to readings of the sagas of Abu Zeid al-Hilal[25] and Antara bin Shaddad.[26] We became such close friends that I even went with them occasionally to al-Aqsa Mosque for weekly prayer. It was such an experience, and strangely unexpected for someone brought up by strict Lutheran Protestant parents.

This pleasant existence was abruptly interrupted by the rise in hostilities between Palestinian Arabs and Jews. It was around this time that the rebellion of 'Izz al-Din al-Qassam[27] began in central and north Palestine, before spreading. When Qassam was killed[28] in a major battle with the British Army, the Higher Arab Committee – made up of notables from all communities in Palestine, including Palestinian political parties, and headed by the Grand Mufti of Jerusalem – called the 1936 strike, which lasted for six months. It felt like an eternity and our daily lives were punctured by curfews imposed by the British rulers.

When Jewish products were boycotted collectively, the British began to detain Palestinian activists, and even people found carrying penknives were prosecuted. The Jewish population, meanwhile, was storing more and more weapons and training their fighters. Even before these events, I had developed a deep ideological belief in Arab nationalism as the best way to counter the Zionist threat.[29]

By that time, I had met Sami al-Ansari, a handsome young man who became one of my best friends. He was so distressed by the British dealings with the Arab population, and decided to take part in the attempt to assassinate the British Police Commander in Jerusalem. The attempt failed and Sami was shot dead by the guards. He was buried like a hero, and I grieved for him for months afterwards. The 1930s were now coming to an end and the rebellion was crushed brutally by the British, who proposed what was known as the White Paper in 1939[30] which suggested the establishment of a joint Jewish–Arab state, the capping of Jewish migration and access to land. Land sales were to be prohibited unless approved by the High Commissioner. But the paper was rejected by both parties outright. I really don't know whether that was wise.

I was by then teaching at *al-Umariyya*, a school affiliated with the highly esteemed Arab College[31] that used to train teachers who later were enlisted to work with the Department of Education. I had become attached to teaching and enjoyed my work, but the growing hostilities and the feeling that something was about to happen made me feel restless and frustrated. I could not afford to stop working because I was responsible for my widowed mother and two siblings, though I wanted to be more active politically. It was frustrating.

In the summer of 1942, I went to visit Haifa and Nazareth, my home town in the north, and then went on to Jaffa for inspiration, but nothing could lift my spirits. At that time, news of Jewish attacks on Palestinian homes brought home the rising threat. Palestinian armed groups struck back intermittently, but were repressed by the British rulers. In Jerusalem, we heard that the Haganah[32] militia was planning to launch an attack on the western, northern and eastern sides of the city. The Qatamon suburb in the south-west, where I lived at the time, was nightly shaken by the sound of exploding bombs,[33] in preparation for a takeover. One night, the gigantic Semiramis Hotel collapsed to the ground. It was attacked because of Jewish claims that it was the meeting place of Arab activists and fighters. We lived less than half a kilometre [quarter of a mile] away and the explosion woke us up, and so we decided to move to Bethlehem for safety. That was a few months before Jewish troops occupied the western, Arab part of the city, after months of heavy shelling and random attacks.

I used to make my way to Jerusalem daily, leaving in the early morning and coming back late in the evening. At the beginning, this was easy as I was able to go by car, but when the situation in Jerusalem deteriorated, the attacks on the roads increased, and cars and buses stopped running, I started going with a colleague on his motorbike. After two months, the highway became too dangerous because of sniper fire from a Jewish settlement on the way and I decided to board at the college. I was given a room which I shared with a fellow teacher at the college. It was difficult to get much sleep because of the sound of machine guns and explosions in front-line areas not far from the college. Strangely enough, my room-mate always slept soundly.

It is hard to remember all the details, but when the British Mandate[34] came to an end and the roads were inaccessible, I could no longer make the journey. The massacre of Deir Yassin took place on 8 April 1948, causing widespread flight and fright. At least 300 villagers were killed and the news of the assault spread fear to many villagers.[35] On 15 May 1948, Israel was established, and with the expansion of the Jewish onslaught and aggression, neighbouring Arab states were dragged into war. Though I was safe, the loss was such a personal blow that I felt I could not cope with the occupation. I bade farewell to my friends and family and made my way to Damascus to apply for a teaching post in Syria. My move was voluntary, but I was an exile, like many others, without any home to call my own for most of my life.[36]

A homeland has no borders: Sa'id Barghouti's story[37]

The writing was on the wall, but we did not know this and we did not understand what it meant. I was a child in the early 1940s, but even today I can still see the slogan on the walls of Safad: 'Down with the Balfour Declaration.' At the time, I did not know the extent of the threat of Zionism or what was going on; nor did many others at that time. In fact, thinking about it now, there was no real grass-roots awareness of the extent of the danger of that declaration, but the Jews knew what it meant and they were preparing the ground-work for their takeover of Palestine. In fact, we later learned they had prepared about 25,000 soldiers for the takeover.

Nobody told me what the revolutionaries were supposed to be doing. Nobody really talked about this, but we all knew there was a group of *mujahideen*, armed and camouflaged men, who kept guard along the road leading to the Jewish quarter in the city and engaged in armed conflict against the British. I was born in 1938, in the middle of the Great Revolt. I was a curious child, always asking questions, but it is strange how I never got answers to the questions that bothered me. For example, I often wondered why sandbags were placed at the windows and balconies of a building situated at the entrance to the Jewish quarter to the city. There was a bakery, too. Perhaps the Jews living there knew that something was about to happen and were preparing.

Our house was in the village of Sidr,[38] just outside Safad. It was a large house by the standards of the day, perhaps the largest in the village, and was surrounded by its own garden. In the summer, we slept on the roof, and my mother, always concerned about our health, would come up with extra blankets. The land was the centre of our universe, the focus of our identification. It is strange what one remembers, but I can clearly see my headmaster, Shafiq al-Brik, wearing what we called the *faisaliya*, a form of head-dress named after King Faisal,[39] who was rumoured to be fond of it. I cannot think why the name and face of this headmaster remains etched in my memory. Our garden was abundant with trees that my father had planted himself in 1937, a year before my birth. My favourite was a pomegranate tree that had grown in such a way that it formed the perfect seat for me to sit on and read for hours. We often hosted weddings in a large hall in the house that was called *thulthiyya* – so named because it was a third of the area of the house. It was the perfect room for happy occasions.

Those are snapshots of my life I shall always remember, and there are also other moments, including the moment when our lives collapsed. The day this happened started at school in the morning, when our teacher came to class and told us to go home. We were delighted to be let off and almost ran home. And yet, even before then, I would overhear the elders speaking about the fighting that had escalated between the Jewish and Arab populations, particularly when the Haganah intensified rocket attacks on Safad,[40] launching mortar bombs and terrorizing the inhabitants. The shooting was arbitrary, coming from all directions, and causing widespread fear and confusion. One of the bombs was lobbed into a market place and killed 13 Arabs, mostly children.

On that fateful afternoon, my mother came to find me and told me to come bid my uncle's family goodbye as they were leaving for Damascus. My uncle's wife was a sensitive woman with a child around my age. She took one look at me and realized that I was envious and that I too wanted to go along. I thought they were going on a holiday and I did not want to be left behind. She read my mind just by looking in my eyes. As we were leaving, she asked: 'Sa'id, my dear, do you want to go with us?' I looked at my mother, who immediately said: 'If you want to go, go with your uncle's wife and your cousin.' And that's how I left to this exile.

We left on foot and walked until we arrived at this village at sunset and sought shelter in the house of the *mukhtar* [the head of the village]. I really cannot remember the name of this village, nor can I find it on a map even now. He offered us a place to sleep and it was when I put my head on the pillow and tried to sleep that I felt this intense sadness and fright. I wanted my mother. All I could do was cover my head with a blanket and weep in silence.

I was still in tears the next morning when we took a car to Quneitra on the border with Syria. Then we boarded a bus to Damascus. I sat next to another child who appeared to be on his own, and I was curious to find out if he was indeed alone without his mother. So I asked him whether his mother was with him, hoping he would say no and I would not feel so alone, but he said she was sitting at the front of the bus. I tell you this story because it remains vivid in my brain to this day. It meant much more than longing for my mother, who arrived a few days later. It meant longing for normality, for a way of life that was lost for good. My father followed soon after, having given up resisting the Jewish onslaught. When he arrived, all I could ask was whether he brought the cat, Ghazal ['deer'], with him. And he said: 'Don't worry, *Yaba*:[41] I left two broken eggs for him on a plate to eat.'

In exile, the talk was about return, which became a nightmare. The younger generation was divided ideologically, wondering which political grouping to join and there was not much awareness of politics or its meaning at the time. I myself joined the Arab Nationalist Movement in 1956 because they had big ideas and dreams, and because of the hope that the idea of unity (between Syria and Egypt) created. I remember how some of us went to this camp to be trained by the Syrians to carry out acts of resistance against Israel. It was led by a well-known Syrian officer, Akram al-Safadi. I joined and was upgraded to become an officer in 1961.[42]

Remembering is so difficult, and it makes me emotional to think about how we ended up here. I have a relative, called Fady, who spent his childhood and adulthood in Safad. When he left Palestine, he was 50 years old plus. I went to visit him in hospital when he was almost on his deathbed and he told me one thing I shall always remember. He said: 'You know, Sa'id ... in Safad there are no borders.' And it dawned on me that this is what a homeland is about. Of course, a homeland has no borders.[43]

The peasant past:[44] Salah Salah's story[45]

I am a Bedu, born in 1936 in Ghuwayr abu Shusha,[46] a place that exists to this day. In my mind, it remains the most beautiful place in the world. I know this for certain because I have travelled far and wide: to Europe, China and Latin America.

What remains fixed in my memory is a vision of this place sitting on a hill near a meadow reaching as far as Lake Tiberias. The climate is moderate and pleasant, so it is fertile and green. We used to grow all types of vegetables, as well as grain and wheat, and some fruit trees. There were two Jewish settlements nearby, one an old settlement called al-Majdal,[47] inhabited by the people we called 'the Arab Jews', and the other a settlement called Genossar.

Ours was one of those rare places with two distinct seasons, summer and winter. There were eight to nine *hamulas* ['clans'], each with its own chief, who formed what we call a 'council of clans' that met to solve problems. One chief was called Abu Muwahash; he solved everyday problems and his decisions were taken seriously. My uncle, the eldest amongst his brothers, was the chief of our clan. He owned a large plot of land which later was considered as lost property.

We always ate together, a tradition that continued until 1948, when we left Palestine and carried on the same customs. Our lives were contained somehow. Everybody knew everyone else; we knew who was in charge and we did not have to go to court or to state institutions to resolve family disputes. We only went to the courts when we were in conflict with the neighbouring Jewish communities over who owned the land. Land disputes became increasingly contentious and difficult to resolve. At one stage, I remember, the British came round in jeeps to take a head count and to find out who owned what. The villagers refused to co-operate at first because some were worried about British intentions. But there was little awareness of what politics meant at the time.

There was no school in my village, so I went to learn the Koran and the teachings of Prophet Mohammed from a preacher. When I was old enough, I went to school in the nearby village of al-Majdal. I must have been 12 at that time. We used to take a bus, called *Bas Anqura*, and we often lingered before hopping on so the bus driver would tell us off for making him late, but we enjoyed the walk by the lake through the farms and we wanted to make the most of our time outside before sitting down to do some work. We had two teachers who told us about the meaning of Communism and its attraction as an ideology, but at that time, such talk was difficult for a Bedu who felt he was an Arab. Then, becoming a Communist felt like peeling off my skin.

In 1939, when the Palestinian revolt was in its last gasps, the British forces raided our village because they suspected we had collaborated with the *mujahideen* and had hidden their weapons. My father refused to go when they ordered all men to go with them and leave the women behind. He thought he could protect himself. They threatened him by pointing a pistol at his head and insisted on interrogating him, so he suffered a breakdown and died after we took him to the hospital in Tiberias. That's how he died. I can never forget that.

We kept good relations with the neighbouring Arab Jews, with whom we used to trade. There was no hostility to speak of at the beginning, but clashes erupted when we could no longer resolve the disputes over land and when some outsider Jews began to appear in large numbers and with arms. We, on the other hand, had fewer than 12 guns to protect us and people used primitive means to defend against attacks when these took place. For example, the villagers would shoot from one place and move to another so that the attackers would think there were more people fighting and more weapons to fight with. Twelve guns can make a lot of noise! Another method was to rattle empty containers to cause anxiety and disturbance.

Of course, this was at the beginning, but then everything was turned upside down when we started hearing news of villages falling and people running away. When we heard that Tiberias had fallen, followed by Safad, we began to have doubts about our ability to fight back and to protect ourselves. It was then that the decision to leave was taken to protect the people. We left to a village called al-Rameh and from there to Lebanon. The scenes of departure are unforgettable because there were many people walking in different directions, overlapping, crossing each other, but all leaving. It was a massive exodus. I cannot describe how I felt.

Like many other Palestinians, we thought we would be going back so we only took some coffee pots with us to make coffee. Drinking coffee was central to our social activities and this custom continued in the early days of our lives as refugees. It was a joy to sit with the elders, even in the camps, and listen to stories about Palestine. When Suleiman Baker brought a newspaper for us to read, I began to be fascinated by news and I volunteered to distribute newspapers to my friends and fellow students at school.

With this, I developed a good relationship with the publisher, who introduced me to Muhsin Ibrahim, one of the great icons of the Lebanese National Movement at the time, and I soon persuaded my friends to form a small group affiliated to the Arab Nationalist

Movement. Those were some of the most beautiful years in my life because it was the beginning of the grassroots foundations of the Palestinian revolution.

In those early days as refugees, we felt ashamed, frustrated and dispossessed, so the idea that we, as young people, could motivate others was uplifting and liberating. Those were the 1950s, when I was a young man who wanted to confront defeat and move on. I had this absolute commitment to organize and mobilize people, so we started forming youth clubs in secret and it was through the need to reach out to others that we began to go to other places, like Beirut and Sidon. The mobilization was necessary because, at that time, there was talk of the Palestinian problem as a refugee problem and there were all these proposals for naturalization and settlement of the refugees, even in remote parts of the Arab world. We did not have much money, but we felt the people were behind us. It was a period of real struggle and clean revolution.

'I called my daughter Sourriyya': Um Thabet's story[48]

I called my daughter *Sourriyya* [Syria] because that's where we ended up. They [the Jewish militias] terrified us and chased us out, so we ended up here. As we arrived in the tent, my daughter was born. She was such a beautiful child, with lovely blonde hair and blue eyes, and I decided to register her at school at the age of five. I wanted all my children to have an education, and they all did. I had five girls before I started having boys. In total, I gave birth to seven boys and seven girls. I used to have a child every year.

We were fine here in the camps, living like everyone else, but we always talked about Palestine and told our children about life there, about the fig trees, about the olive trees and the grapevines. They also heard stories about Palestine from the other refugees and they would come and tell me off for not telling them more stories about the good life, but it was hard to think about it or talk about

1   Um Thabet sitting in her house at Yarmouk Camp, Damascus, showing a picture of herself and her daughter to her grandchildren. Photograph: Tanya Habjouqa.

it when we had to make a living from nothing and get on with our lives.

You know, I dream of Palestine all the time. I see the olive trees so clearly and the grass on which we used to sit to eat figs after a day's work in the fields. We, the girls and the women, worked the fields and tended the orchards, just like the men. In fact, besides normal domestic work and childcare, we women dried and stored the foodstuffs which the families used for winter, such as grains, pulses, olives and olive oil.[49] It makes me happy to remember and I feel I am alive again.

We lived in the village of Ja'ouneh[50] in upper Galilee. Our house was a short walk from the Jewish district. The butcher next door was a Jew who warned my father of the impending danger, but we never took him seriously, except one day when he said: 'Some of these new Jews [the migrants] will provoke you and ask you to leave.' That was when the problems began. Up to then, life was about growing plants, cooking, looking after livestock, getting married, bringing up children and socializing. We grew beans, okra, tomatoes, figs and watermelon. Some of my friends went back to visit and I begged them to pass by my village and bring me a handful of earth, and they told me how beautiful it still is.

In those days, we heard stories about the *mujahideen* (revolutionaries) who took part in the revolt (1936–9), but we did not meet any of them. I heard about 'Izz al-Din al-Qassam from my mother, who also taught us *ahajeez* ['songs'] about him and other revolutionaries hiding in the mountains of Canaan. We sang for him and for other revolutionaries, to Fouad Hijazi, Muhammad Jamjoum and Abu Ibrahim. Those three were given the death penalty. I used to have a beautiful voice and I shall sing you the song:

> *Wa min sijen 'Akka tala't janazi*
> *Muhammad Jumjum wa Fu'ad Hijazi*
> *Wa jazi' alayhum ya sha'abi jazi*
> *Mandub al-sami wa rub'ahu amuma*

> [A funeral procession went from Acre prison
> For Muhammad Jumjum and Fu'ad Hijazi.
> He punished them, O people,
> The High Commissioner and his people punished them.][51]

Our best days were the days when we celebrated happy events like weddings. All the people would gather, singing the *a'ataba* and *meyjana* (folkloric songs or chants), and dancing the *dabke* (group dance). We would prepare masses of food and made *lawziya*, sweets filled with almonds, sugar and then mixed with olive oil. We used to make cookies and other sweets that had Turkish names, like *zarad* and *zunqul*. We put on our finest clothes on wedding days, and our Jewish neighbours who lived nearby would tell us that they had never seen such beautiful women, even in Europe! The bride would normally stay at her uncle's house the night before the wedding. She would put on a red dress on the wedding day and then go on horseback to the groom's home, followed by women singing behind. At that time, the bridegroom would be taking part in the *sahja*, being led round the village, then to the threshing floor and then to his house on horseback.

I stayed at my maternal uncle's house before I got married. I was only 13 and the wedding day was the first time I saw my husband-to-be. My mother had not prepared me for what happens, but I had heard that if the groom were good-natured and came from a good family, he would chat up the bride and soften her heart on that evening. And that's what happened. Abu Yousef chatted to me and softened my heart because he is a good, kind man.

I cannot describe my *dar* ['house'] to you because it is just an image, but it was a house of stone built around four columns. So it must have been square. My father used to take me with him to Nazareth and Nablus for visits. We lived together, I mean the boys and the girls, but I was so envious of the boys who went to school and I would often stand at the window outside the classroom listening to what the teacher had to say. I heard the boys repeating Koranic verses. I dreamt of the day when I would be treated the same way, but that never happened because things came to a halt all of a sudden.

I cannot remember the sequence of events and when exactly or why we decided to leave. I had three children and all I could think of at the time was where to sleep with my three little girls and, on waking up, where to go. I had to protect them because I saw with my own eyes armed Jewish men coming down from the mountains and the women running around terrified with no shoes on. We had heard how they had attacked other women and children in nearby villages and we were scared.

After three days sleeping in the wild, I went back with my husband to the village to collect some bread and food and I left the girls behind. When I came back I realized that one of my daughters, Mariam, was missing. I almost went mad with fear and I ran around trying to find her, forgetting about the others. It was then that a man came to me and asked me whether I had lost a child and that's how I found her. I could have almost lost one of my children in that chaos. It would have been too much, following the loss of the land and our home.

I sleep with a dagger under my belt: Um Salah's story[52]

Nobody leaves their home of their own free will. This was forced on us. We had to leave our village, Hajur,[53] during the war. Back then, we did everything with our own hands, everything. Today, you have to buy everything. Nothing comes directly from the land itself. I had three children with me when we left: one boy was six, the other four and the youngest, a few months old, I carried on my back. We left with everyone else, arriving in Halhul near Hebron, before ending up here in Bethlehem. In Halhul, we stayed for 12 days, with no water or food. Nothing, except what we had managed to carry by hand.

In our village, we used to grow wheat and all sorts of vegetables. Our trees bore the best fruit. Nothing tastes the same as the produce from your homeland, where there are hills and trees and where hearts are clear and open. Here, you are fenced and enclosed, and your heart is black with fear. I sleep with a dagger under my belt out of fear, even to this very day. I cannot forget what happened in 2002 at the height of the second Palestinian *intifada*. My grandson came and woke me up then and said 'The Israelis are demolishing some houses!' They came on us all of a sudden and put us in one room. Then they killed my daughter-in-law. I heard her screaming. They [the Israelis] can come anytime. Whenever I watch the news on television, I remember all these events and I feel sad, and terrified. Really, if you ask me what I want. I want peace with the Jews. I pray this happens each day.

Our village was one of the last villages to fall. It was flooded with refugees fleeing the fighting in other parts of Palestine. And that was when our life changed. You know, we used to feel so secure and safe that we, even the young girls, slept outdoors. We could go anywhere on our own, tend to the fields, look after the cows and sheep. There was nothing to fear, really. No Jews lived nearby, but the English and some Jordanians used to call on the village sometimes.

I keep telling my children and grandchildren these stories. I tell them about our weddings and the beautiful, embroidered clothes we used to wear then. Brides these days look so different, and not as pretty. My husband is a relative of mine who had heard about me and he came to ask for my hand. I was told I was beautiful those days. Life was so beautiful, with no restrictions, unlike today. This camp is a prison, a cage. I cannot walk in the valley or in the green fields. I can barely see the sun.

Thoughts of paradise: Abu 'Arab's story of Saffuriyyeh[54]

I met Abu 'Arab in his shop, in the old market in Nazareth, in November 2007. He is a political activist, committed to keeping the memory of pre-1948 Saffuriyyeh alive while maintaining pressure on Israel by commemorative events[55] and campaigns to reclaim some of the land. Nazareth remains largely Arab and is the largest place of residence for Palestinian internal refugees. The majority of its inhabitants fled during the July 1948 bombing or in the later expulsions. Though some people returned, a final expulsion order in 1949 forced them out to surrounding villages or into exile, and the village was declared a military zone.

I was 12 when the Zionists occupied my land, when my village fell. I was probably in the 5th grade. Saffuriyyeh was a prosperous village, with some 4,500 people and 55,000 *dunums* [55 sq. km/21 sq. ml] of fertile land. We had plenty of water and green fields which people farmed. Each family owned a bit of land to grow crops on. We had two schools, one for boys and the other for girls. There were three mosques and eight olive factories. We traded with nearby Nazareth and Haifa, selling them vegetables. Maybe four to five people served in the British Army under the Mandate; one was Ahmad al-Tubi. They wore uniforms and owned cars, and some even had some guns. But, when the fighting with the Jews began, it was the peasants who led the resistance.

We came under air attack on the 16th day of the fasting month of Ramadan. The attacks came out of the blue and the ground shook with the explosions. My mother was making *mloukhiya* [a green stew, popular in Egypt, made of plant leaves similar to spinach] when we heard a plane flying overhead, and then the bombs began to fall. Of course, it was nothing like what happens these days, but it felt like nuclear bombs then. We had no underground bunkers to hide in.

The decision to leave under such ferocious and sustained attack was made so suddenly that we could snatch only a few belongings. As we fled up the hill, I looked back and all I could see was smoke. We knew the village had fallen, but the Palestinians did not give up elsewhere, because fighting continued in the north. Our parents were simple people and all they wanted was to protect their children. I don't blame them, but we have to continue fighting for our rights.

Along with hundreds of others, we walked north until we reached Bint Jbeil in Lebanon, where some of our relatives were waiting with blankets and food. We stayed there for 28 days, and then we boarded some buses which took us to an area called *al-Saha al-Hamra* ['the red square'] before going off to the Bekaa' [Valley], where we stayed in makeshift tents for 11 months before renting a house.

Those were such miserable days. My sister, who was one year younger than me, became sick and died within weeks. The house we lived in overlooked the cemetery where she was buried, and my mother never stopped mourning and crying, so that my father said she had gone mad with grief. It was during that bleak period that we started pondering whether to go on to Beirut or return to Palestine. Having heard that many other villagers from Saffuriyyeh had gone to Nazareth and that job prospects there were good, we took the decision to head there, becoming internally displaced refugees. That's what they call us now.

Ours was one of about 531 villages destroyed by the Zionists. They confiscated the land and destroyed houses, the planted trees and the orchards, and they tried to change everything. Under military rule, we could not go back and visit without a permit. Now we go but we are not allowed to stay or live there. I believe that one day we will. It might not be me personally, but it will be my son or my grandson.

In fact, this belief in return and getting back what is my right informs my life and experiences here. My life remains a temporary one, even after 60 years. I am here in Nazareth in transit and I do not see myself as an Israeli citizen with equal rights. The Israeli identity card was imposed on me. I never wanted it and I did not choose it. I live in *hay al-Saffuriyyeh* ('the Saffuriyyeh quarter') in the town and, when I look out of my window in the morning, I see my home town. Every morning, I look towards it and I think that it not only represents what Palestine is or was, but it is my *Ka'abeh,* my paradise, my whole reason for being. This thought keeps me alive.[56]

It is a question of belonging: Shafik al-Hout[57]

What follows is an edited version of an interview I had with Shafik al-Hout at his home in Beirut in April 2007. Shafik[58] joined the Palestine Liberation Organization in 1964 and served as its representative in Beirut until his resignation in 1993. His grandfather moved to Jaffa from Lebanon in the last quarter of the nineteenth century, following in the footsteps of his brother who had married a woman from Jaffa and settled there. Boundaries at that time were fluid, and northern Palestine under the Ottomans was part of the Beirut vilayet, so movement and intermarriage were common. The contrast with what happened under colonial rule and then the *Nakba* is telling.

I was born in Jaffa in January 1932. I studied in government schools which, under British rule, were considered to be the best. Then I went to Al-Amiriyah school, one of the most important secondary schools in Palestine. It was ahead of its time because it employed a number of teachers with university degrees from Egypt or Lebanon, which was not a common practice at the time.

It was at school that I developed strong nationalist feelings and, like many of my contemporaries, became involved in politics. One of my teachers who left a good impression on me was Shafik Abu-Arabi, who was martyred while preparing an explosive device in Hebron. He fostered an intense nationalist feeling through his lectures on the threat of Zionism and the dangers of British colonial rule and through the trips we took with him to various parts of Palestine.

Jaffa was the cultural capital of Palestine and, in that respect, possibly more important than Jerusalem was at the time. Many Palestinian newspapers were published in Jaffa, attracting serious intellectuals, writers and journalists. Jaffa was also distinct from other Palestinian cities because of its sensitive geographical location near Tel Aviv, the biggest Zionist colony nearby. Among the newspapers at that time were *Filastin*, published by 'Isa and Yousuf al-'Isa, and *al-Karmil*, edited by Najib Nassar in neighbouring Haifa. *Al-Karmil* was the most outspoken in its opposition to Zionism and became the primary vehicle for an extensive countrywide campaign against Jewish settlement in Palestine, migration which came to a peak in 1911.[59]

We read the papers meticulously and were deeply touched by the poetry that some of these papers published. In fact, we would read these poems out loud to those who could not read at the time. Jaffa also hosted the radio station for the Near East, which would often broadcast Arab writers such as Abbas Mahmoud el-Aqqad and Abdel Rahman al-Khamissy. Most interviews were conducted live, providing fascinating insights into cultural issues. Jerusalem was the political capital because all the political parties were based there, but Jaffa was where all the action happened.

In the Mandate period, it retained its Arab character. The few Jews who arrived in the late 1920s and early 1930s were forced out. Jaffa was not controlled by elite families like the Husseinis and Khalidis in Jerusalem or the Masris in Nablus. I could really call

Jaffa 'Palestinian cosmopolitan' as well as Arab, because a lot of people in Jaffa were of Lebanese descent. Relations between Arab Christians and Muslims were good. My older brother, for example, became a member of the Christian Orthodox club.

I lived in a neighbourhood separated from Tel Aviv[60] by a football field, which soon turned into a battleground for stone-throwing matches between us and the Jews. We rarely played them, I mean at real sports. In fact, we Palestinians often felt uncomfortable in Tel Aviv and, if ever we ventured in just half a kilometre into the streets of Tel Aviv, they would start screaming: 'It's an Arab, Arab!'

I grew up at a time of political parties, like the Defence Party and the Reform Party, similar to political parties today in terms of structure and rules. But I was more closely involved with the Communist Party because it was the most organized, plus I was inspired by its ideology and its commitment to getting rid of the British. In my teens, politics took up most of my time, because even at that young age I was conscious that we needed to mobilize and infiltrate schools to agitate for action among young people. Whenever a demonstration was planned, we would visit schools to mobilize students to join, so that, by the time we reached the heart of the city, we would be about 5,000 to 6,000 strong. We timed our demonstrations to take place around prayer time so people would come out of the large mosque in the main square in Jaffa and join in.

At home, our life was conservative. My mother used to wear a black headscarf and traditional dress. Although men and women mixed, this was only within the family and among close friends. There was a girls' school right opposite ours and it was often a matter of great excitement and endless chatter whenever one of us, teenagers at the time, spotted a girl across the street. In those days, we did not talk about sex with our parents or teachers unless it had to do with what was *halal* or *haram* ['permissible' or 'not allowed']. Our main event in the school year was Sports Day which we would prepare for throughout the year. It was a wonderful day. Matches were mostly between Palestinian teams from

Haifa and Jerusalem, and, on rare occasions, against a Jewish team.

Jaffa had an organization which would put on social and cultural events, on such special occasions as *Mawlid al-Nabi* ['the birth of the prophet']. It would also oversee the spring festival celebrations when people would go to the beach south of Jaffa. These were most of the activities that were around at that time. In the holidays in the spring and during the Muslim feasts, we would go cycling, to *Areeha* [Jericho] and other villages.

Even then, I used to feel astonished at the difference between the Arab villages and the Israeli settlements. They seemed to have much more. We saw films in those days, but we frequented the cinema in Tel Aviv because this had a wider screen and showed a variety of films. The cinemas in Jaffa mainly screened Egyptian movies. I still remember to this day the streets of Tel Aviv.

My father became involved in armed resistance and was assassinated in 1948. We had no choice but to leave, particularly when rumours reached us about the ruthless nature of the Jewish attacks. We left, like many other Jaffans, thinking we would be back within days or weeks. We were so convinced about this that we rented furnished accommodation for three years because we still had our home in Jaffa. We left on 24 April 1948. Reflecting on this, I realize that there had been no organization nor enough awareness to resist this collective forced exodus. We carried a few possessions, mostly clothes, but we knew we had relatives across the border who would take us in. It was approaching summer, and I, like others, thought we would be spending the summer in Beirut. It was only after the passage of a number of years that we knew the road back was going to be long.

What can you say to someone whose 'normal' existence has been taken away from him? It took me a while to have a bed and a room to call my own. It might not seem that hard to you, but believe me living in a room with so many people for eight years is hell. And yet it is nothing compared to others' experiences. I have been through a lot and you can read about my experiences and my journey to exile in my book. And, now that I am an old man and more reflective, I can tell you that my experiences taught me that no matter what life throws at you, you can survive. You can survive loss, but you cannot get over this void, the void of not-belonging. It is not a question of land, but of not-belonging.

Notes

1. For an extensive account of memories of the revolt, see Ted Swedenburg (2003) *Memories of Revolt: The 1936–39 Rebellion and the Palestinian National Past*, Fayetteville: University of Arkansas Press.
2. Swedenburg, *Memories of Revolt.*
3. Ilan Pappé (2006) *The Ethnic Cleansing of Palestine*, Oxford: Oneworld Publications.
4. No marker commemorates al-Qassam's death at the site of the famous battle near the West Bank of Ya'bad, west of Jenin, but the site is still remembered by many residents. Qassam's grave is in Balad al-Shaikh (now Nesher), near Haifa.
5. Yezid Sayigh (1997) *Armed Struggle and the Search for State: The Palestinian National Movement, 1949–1993*, Oxford: Oxford University Press.
6. Theodor Herzl (1960) *The Complete Diaries of Theodor Herzl*, Volume 1, New York: Herzl Press, quoted in Ahmad Sa'di (2007) 'Reflections on representation, history and moral accountability' [afterword] in Ahmad Sa'di and Lila Abu-Lughod (eds), *Nakba: Palestine, 1948, and the Claims of Memory*, New York: Columbia University Press.
7. Sayigh, *Armed Struggle and the Search for State.*
8. Although Israeli revisionist historians, such as Benny Morris, began to refute the official Israeli narrative that the Palestinians left 'of their own accord', it was a Palestinian scholar, Nur Masalha, who documented the systematic policy of transfer that was part and parcel of Zionist policies to depopulate Palestine from the start; see Nur Masalha (1992) *Expulsion of the Palestinians: The Concept of 'Transfer' in Zionist Political Thought, 1882–1948*, Washington, DC: Institute for Palestine Studies.
9. Rashid Khalidi (1997) *Palestinian Identity: The Construction of Modern National Consciousness*, New York: Columbia University Press.
10. The figure of 531 villages is used by Ilan Pappé in his work on the *Nakba*; see Pappé, *Ethnic Cleansing.* Note that Abu-Sitta's

extensive research on the destroyed settlements included 77 Bedouin villages in the Beersheba area in the total. See Salman Abu-Sitta (2004) *Atlas of Palestine, 1948*, London: Palestine Land Society.

11. An UNRWA report of 1951 stated there were 875,998 refugees registered. Salman Abu-Sitta suggests a figure of 935,000.

12. For an extensive reading of the revolt, based on interviews with elderly villagers who took part in this significant event, see Swedenburg, *Memories of Revolt.*

13. For work on oral history and the *Nakba*, see Sa'di and Abu-Lughod, *Nakba: Palestine, 1948.*

14. The beauty of the Palestinian landscape is often evoked in poems, particularly in the resistance poetry of Mahmoud Darwish, Samih al-Qassem and Tawfik Zayyad, which came from inside Israel and began to find its way outside after 1967.

15. Baruch Kimmerling and Joel S. Migdal (1994/2003) *The Palestinian People: A History*, Cambridge, MA: Harvard University Press.

16. Sa'di and Abu-Lughod, *Nakba: Palestine, 1948.*

17. Samera Esmier (2003) 'Law, history, memory', *Social Text*, 21/2, pp. 25–48.

18. Fawaz Turki (1988) *Soul in Exile: Lives of a Palestinian Revolutionary*, New York: Monthly Review Press.

19. Rosemary Sayigh (1979/2007) *The Palestinians: From Peasants to Revolutionaries*, London: Zed Books.

20. Ilan Pappé (2004/2006) *A History of Modern Palestine*, Cambridge: Cambridge University Press.

21. See Beshara Doumani (1995) *Rediscovering Palestine: Merchants and Peasants in Jabal Nablus, 1700–1900*, Berkeley: California University Press, for an account of the importance of other cities, such as Nablus and Hebron, as trade centres during most of the nineteenth century.

22. Khalidi (1997) *Palestinian Identity.*

23. Henry Matar was 18 when he moved from Nazareth to Jerusalem to take up a teaching post in 1934, two years before the revolt began. This is an edited account of his story, which he wrote in 1992, one year before he died. It was not possible for me to interview him further about various elements or to press him for more details. As a written account, it is qualitatively different from all the other verbal stories. His was definitely influenced by his wide reading and knowledge of political developments later on in life. I wanted to include it to show that even for someone with a

relatively more educated, though from a lower middle-class background, he was not politically aware of events until he went to Jerusalem and had contacts with other people who were more motivated at the time and until real events made him conscious of politics.

24. In fact, many of those interviewed told of how Muslims and Christians, and even Jews, co-existed in the same neighbourhood.

25. Abu Zeid al-Hilal was a tenth-century Arab leader and Islamic hero.

26. Antara ibn Shaddad was a pre-Islamic Ethiopian poet and hero. His best poems are contained in the *Mu'allaqat*, which form the basis of a long and extravagant romance.

27. Most Palestinians interviewed knew that al-Qassam was born in what is now Syria, not Palestine, and that he took refuge in Palestine in the early 1920s after he was sentenced to death by the French authorities for his role in resisting the French occupation. He remains one of the many images of insurgency ingrained in Palestinian minds, with the potential to inspire struggle against colonial domination. .

28. No marker commemorates al-Qassam's death at the site of the famous battle near the West Bank of Ya'bad, west of Jenin, but the site is still remembered by many residents.

29. I did not have the chance to ask my father how he developed this ideological belief, but – as many scholars, notably Rashid Khalidi, have commented – newspapers in Cairo, Beirut and Damascus drew attention to Zionist practices. These concerns were picked up by newspapers in Palestine, which either wrote editorials or reprinted in full the original articles. Khalidi's argument (in his book *Palestinian Identity*) goes further back in time, suggesting that the period between 1899 and 1914 reflected an explicit awareness of the threat. Khalidi sees this as a Palestinian example of the kind of imagined community whose members share a body of knowledge and a consciousness of belonging to one entity.

30. The White Paper, approved by a comfortable majority of Parliament in London on 17 May 1939, rejected the idea of partitioning Palestine and creating a separate Jewish state there; the British government declared itself in favour of limiting Jewish immigration to Palestine to 75,000 annually for the next five years ad of creating an independent Palestinian state within a decade, to be governed jointly, on a proportional basis, by Arabs and Jews.

The paper was opposed by the Zionist movement which mobilized all its means and allies to counter it, beginning a radical phase in its operations against the mandatory authority in Palestine. The rejection by the Higher Arab Committee, representing or speaking on behalf of the Palestinian national movement, was less understandable. In fact, as Bayan Nuwayhid al-Hout reports, citing accounts by the participants, 'a majority of the members of the Committee had approved the White Paper after discussing it in detail at a special meeting held in Qurnayil (the residence of the Jerusalem Mufti in Lebanon); the Mufti (Haj Amin al-Husseini) rejected it because of the ambiguity of its clauses,' (see al-Hout, *Bayan Nuwayhid*, [Al-Qiyadat was al-Mu'assasat al'Siyasiyya fi Filastin], 1917–1948, Beirut: Mu'assasat al-Dirasat al-Filastiniyya, 1981).

31. The Arab College was the top state school in the country, and there was fierce competition for each of the 100 places there each year.

32. The Jewish paramilitary organization that later became the core of the Israeli Defence Force.

33. Qatamon fell in the last days of April. In all, 8 Palestinian suburbs and 39 villages were ethnically cleansed in the Greater Jerusalem area, and their population was transferred to the eastern part of the city, following heavy shelling and attacks, which forced some of the richer Palestinian inhabitants out of the town. For further details on demolished and depopulated villages, see Pappé, *Ethnic Cleansing*.

34. British rule did not so much draw to a close as collapse under the weight of domestic turmoil. Assassinations, attacks and kidnappings by the Irgun prompted the evacuation of some British civilians in January 1947 and martial law in parts of the country. By the summer of 1947, the violence was becoming intolerable.

35. Deir Yassin was a small village on the outskirts of Jerusalem that was not involved in any non-Jewish activity. On the morning of 9 April, about 130 Jews from the Irgun and Stern Gang, supported by machine-gun fire from the official Jewish militia, the Haganah, attacked the village, destroying houses and killing the inhabitants as they tried to flee. Those who could not flee were rounded up, taken to a nearby quarry and murdered. One Jewish observer wrote that whole families were killed, while Irgun men raped a number of Arab girls and murdered them.

36. Henry Matar later joined the BBC Arabic Service in London, before going back to Amman for a long career as an educator.

He was an ardent supporter of the Arab Nationalist Party and believed Arab unity was the only way to secure the liberation of Palestine. However, he did not join any political party, but expressed his views in writing, including an unpublished play. He died in Amman in December 1993, still an exile.

37. Sa'id Barghouti (2007). Personal interview with author, Damascus: August.
38. I could not verify the name of the village, but a number of Palestinian villages around Safad were demolished completely.
39. King Faisal, the son of Sharif Hussein (King of Hijaz, 1917–24), was a leading figure in the revolt against the Ottomans. See Kimmerling and Migdal (1994/2003) *The Palestinian People: A History.*
40. Ilan Pappé writes that the battle over Safad began in the middle of April 1948 and that it was tactical considerations, rather than the stubborn resistance from the Palestinians or the Arab Liberation Army, that directed the Jewish campaign first against the rural hinterland around Safad, instead of the town itself. Safad fell on 11 May. Its inhabitants had left for Syria and Lebanon weeks before, after the Jewish armed militias had conquered two villages nearby, to prevent them being used as bases. They took dozens of prisoners and expelled any women, children and old men who tried to stay behind. Later on, the prisoners were murdered in a gully between the villages and Safad. See Pappé, *Ethnic Cleansing.*
41. *Yaba* means 'father'. This way of speaking – parents using their own 'name' (Father or Mother) to address their children – is a dominant form of address in the Arab World. People in the countryside use the forms *Yaba* and *Yamma;* in the towns they use *Baba* and *Mama.*
42. For details of the experiences of the Palestinian battalion in the Syrian Army, see Khalil Jindawi's story in Chapter Three.
43. In Algeria, Sa'id Barghouti went to work at the Palestinian representative office in Algeria, alongside Fatah official Khalil al-Wazir (Abu Jihad). He then went to Libya, from which he was deported for political activities. Barghouti returned to Syria in 1966.
44. All the stories in this section portray the profound sociability of Palestinian peasant life, the simplicity of everyday life and the importance of joyous occasions, such as weddings.
45. Salah Salah (2008). Personal interview with the author, Beirut: August.
46. The village of Ghuwayr was the first village to fall, of a number of villages along the Tiberias–Safad highway. According to Ilan

Pappé, the operation to take over the villages in Safad's hinterland was given the codename *Matateh* ('broom'). See Pappé, *Ethnic Cleansing.*

47. Al-Majdal is now known as Migdal, as part of the Zionist policy to de-Arabize villages and towns in Palestine.

48. Um Thabet (2008) personal interview with the author. Yarmouk Camp/Damascus: August.

49. Rosemary Sayigh has extensively documented the role of peasant woman in pre-*Nakba* Palestine. For details, see Sayigh (1979/2007) *The Palestinians.*

50. I could not find a record of the village of Ja'ouneh.

51. Um Thabet, like many Palestinians, was vague on the historical details of their deaths. In his book on memories of the revolt, Ted Swedenburg says that some people he interviewed thought that the three were involved in the 1936–9 revolt. He later found out that the song was written by Nuh Ibrahim, a popular poet and a fighter in the revolt, and that these three national 'martyrs' (al-Zayr, Jumjum and Hijazi) were convicted of murder for their part in the 1929 massacres of 133 Orthodox Jews in Hebron and Safad.

52. Um Salah (2007). Personal interview with the author, Aida Camp/Bethlehem: April. Um Salah was 85 years old at the time of the interview.

53. Um Salah insisted that she had given me the correct name for the village, Hajur, which I could not trace, but she may have meant al-Huj village in the Gaza/Beersheba area, where former Israeli Prime Minister Ariel Sharon later built his ranch.

54. The Galilee village of Saffuriyyeh was the largest in the region. It was famous in Roman times as Sepphoris. The hilltop has been covered with a pine forest, planted by the Jewish National Fund to cover up signs of any Palestinian past. A travel brochure now welcomes tourists to the ancient Roman ruins, which include an amphitheatre, but it does not mention the capture and ethnic cleansing of the village. The village was attacked from the air and the ground, and occupied by Israeli forces on 15 July 1948. All its inhabitants left, some to neighbouring Nazareth, where they remain today, some of the thousands of internally displaced refugees unable to return to their original homes.

55. Arabs living in Israel form about 18 per cent of the country's population and are commonly referred to as 'Arab Israelis' or 'Israeli Arabs' – a description that goes back to the creation of Israel. Over a million Palestinians hold citizenship in Israel,

descendants of 150,000 Palestinians who remained in the Jewish state following its creation. About a quarter of these people were internally displaced; they were given Israeli identity cards, but not allowed to return to their homes. Palestinians live in segregated Arab towns and villages in northern Galilee, a smaller central 'Triangle' region and the southern Naqab (Negev) desert.

56. The Israeli government has enacted legislation to persuade 'internal refugees' to accept compensation. Few have applied because the offer was not equal to the value of the land lost and the loss of earnings.

57. Shafik al-Hout (2007). Personal interview with author, Beirut: April. Shafik al-Hout passed away on 2 August, 2009, more than two years after I met him.

58. For a full memoir of Shafik al-Hout's life, see his autobiography: Shafik al-Hout (2007) *'Min yafa bada' al-mishwar* ['From Jaffa the journey began'], Beirut: Riyad Rayyes Books.

59. *Filastin* began publishing in 1911, two years after its rival, *al-Karmil*. It became the most important newspaper in the British Mandate, concentrating on education and the peasantry. For more on the Palestinian press, see Khalidi, *Palestinian Identity*.

60. Ilan Pappé says there was an unwritten agreement between Jaffa and Tel Aviv that the two sides would maintain a strip of no-man's land along the coast to divide them, enabling uneasy co-existence. Without consulting them, Haganah troops entered this area and upset the balance, at a time when the two municipalities were trying to reach a new modus vivendi. See Pappé, *Ethnic Cleansing*.

CHAPTER TWO

Living the *Nakba:* In the 'Perilous Territory of Not-Belonging', 1948–64

Since our history is forbidden, narratives are rare; the story of origins, of home, of nation is underground. When it appears, it is broken, often wayward and meandering in the extreme, always coded, usually in outrageous forms – mock-epics, satires, sardonic parables, absurd rituals – that make little sense to an outsider. Thus Palestinian life is scattered, discontinuous, marked by the artificial and imposed arrangements of interrupted and confined space, by the dislocations and unsynchronized rhythms of disturbed time…. How odd the conjuncture, and yet for Palestinians, how fitting. For where no straight line leads from home to birthplace to school to maturity, all events are accidents, all progress is a digression, all residence is exile. (Edward Said)

Palestinian society was left leaderless and disorganized following the 1947–8 war and the *Nakba* fragmented the social strata still further, breaking up the population geographically and making it difficult for Palestinians to articulate a coherent political narrative. When the first political voices began to emerge in the 1970s, the dispossession of 1948 seemed a *fait accompli*. Israel's military victory allowed its Zionist leaders to continue their attempts to expel the Palestinians to surrounding Arab areas. By the time the rest of Palestine had been carved up into Arab spheres of influence, with King Abdullah's annexation of the West Bank and Egypt's jurisdiction over Gaza, there was no longer a centre of gravity with which to identify, and no landscape to claim, but that of the imagination. By the end of the 1947–8 war, the Palestinian people were divided into three broad geopolitical groupings. In the newly created Israeli state, about 150,000 Palestinians remained, of whom about 30,000 were expelled over the next eight months;[1] about 40,000 others were allowed to return from exile under a family reunification scheme in the 1950s.[2] In October 1948 all remaining Palestinians were placed under military rule, which lasted until 1966.

From its early days, Israel extended formal citizenship to the Palestinians who remained within its borders. This move notwithstanding, Israel also subjected them to a host of subjugating practices, including the introduction of a new label to denote them: the hyphenated construct 'Israeli-Arabs'. All movable and immovable property belonging to refugees was considered abandoned and effectively appropriated, while the Absentees Property Law of 1950 was applied to those Palestinians who had 'left [their] ordinary place of residence in Palestine' during the war, even if only to take temporary refuge in nearby villages or mountains.

The Palestinian Arabs were the invisible people of Israel. Fouzi El-Asmar, in his book *To be an Arab in Israel* writes that to be an

> Arab in Israel is to confront a political reality which excludes *a priori*, by the elementary terms of its motivating *raison d'être*, equal participation of non-Jews, first and foremost the native population of the land: the Palestinian-Arabs. To the extent

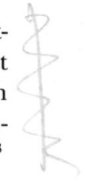

that the state is Jewish it must deny equality of economic, political and national rights to its native non-Jewish population. It
is not incidental that to be an Arab in Israel is to be thrown
into the shadow either as a refugee or as an internally colo-
nised, materially and culturally disinherited 'Arab minority'.[3]

The largest group of Palestinians, about one million
(out of an estimated total of 1.4 million Palestinians overall
in mid-1948), were in the Gaza Strip and the West Bank –
areas seized by Israel in the 1967 Arab–Israeli War. Refugees
in these two areas outnumbered the original residents, with
the disproportion particularly stark in the Gaza Strip, which
welcomed 200,000 refugees on top of its 80,000 original
residents. The third segment, about 300,000 people, fled
beyond Palestinian borders, the majority to Jordan, Lebanon
and Syria, while a smaller number went to Iraq, Libya, Egypt,
Saudi Arabia and Britain. Lebanon and Syria gave the refugees
special cards identifying them as 'Palestinian refugees', but
even middle- and upper-class Palestinians felt they were seen
as foreigners in the eyes of the host countries.

Among the Arab states hosting the bulk of the refugees,
Lebanon imposed the most severe restrictions on the
100,000–130,000 refugees who had arrived by 1949. Lebanese
government policy was shaped to a certain degree by the already
fragile sectarian balance in the country. The Palestinians were
treated as foreigners with regard to employment, investment,
land ownership and white-collar professions. Syria, with 85,000
to 100,000 refugees, freely offered material and moral support,
establishing the Palestine Arab Refugees Institution in 1949
to set up camps and provide general services. Egypt granted
residence to some 7,000 Palestinians and imposed military
administration over Gaza. The Egyptian military authorities, in
control of the Gaza Strip, allowed limited Palestinian activity,
and none that could jeopardize Egypt's armistice agreement
with Israel.[4] In all three states, the Palestinians remained
politically disenfranchised.[5]

Jordan offered its Palestinian inhabitants Jordanian nationality, and parliamentary approval of the Act of Union in April 1950 added nearly 800,000 more Palestinians in the West Bank – 425,000 original residents and 360,000 to 400,000 refugees – and at least 100,000 refugees and 30,000 residents (from before 1948) in the East Bank, on top of the native population of Jordan, then estimated at 340,000.[6] However, the country banned the use of the term 'Palestine' in certain documents, while the Hashemite ruler at the time, King Abdullah, sought to co-opt the 'notables' to control the local population and incorporate the West Bank further into Jordan. Some Palestinians, including those from the established and notable families, went so far as to take on Jordanian identity – not just citizenship, which all Palestinians did at the time. Some of those who ended up in Lebanon did the same, but for different reasons.

In each case, it was the Arab states that determined the political space within which the Palestinians could operate. At the same time, the experience of being socially and politically marginalized effectively transformed 'Palestinian-ism' (to quote Yezid Sayigh) from a 'popular grassroots patriotism' into 'proto-nationalism' in the decade after 1948.[7] Palestinians ultimately made their own choices as to which ideological or organizational group or model to follow, though the means of struggle, timing and opportunities available to them were largely determined by developments in the wider Arab context. By the same token, the creation of the state of Israel and the Palestinian exodus introduced new elements to Arab politics, whereby the post-1948 struggle for power first manifested itself in the struggle over who would represent the Palestinians.[8]

Preserving Palestine

Ghada Karmi, writing about her first years in England after leaving Jerusalem with her family during the *Nakba*, says that no one ever spoke about the circumstances that had prompted their departure from their homeland. Still less did anyone explain to her the history or the politics that lay behind it:

> What private memories, reminiscences, grief, our parents enter-
> tained, we never knew. Palestine had become a faded dream, the
> place of a buried past scarcely ever brought to mind. This played
> directly into my own loss of memory. In some subtle, insensible
> way, I found I had wiped out all remembrance of Jerusalem ….
> This was not a conscious process; I simply put away the past as
> if it had never been. But I wonder if my parents were trying to
> obliterate Palestine from all our memories, partly because they
> could not face recalling the pain and trauma of what had hap-
> pened, but also for another, more hidden reason. Perhaps it was
> a sense of shame for having deserted the homeland, for having
> left it defenceless to the hordes.[9]

Was this constructed amnesia shared by all Palestinians, or was it a myth that fed into discourses of the so-called lost years between 1948 and the emergence of the Palestine Liberation Organization in 1964, when Palestine seemed to have disappeared from the regional political map and from international public discourse, as an independent actor and as a people?[10] The hiatus, Rashid Khalidi[11] argues, can be explained in part by the destruction of Palestinian society and the beginning of a demographic shift with long-lasting consequences, and partly by the powerful ideology of pan-Arabism. This, the hegemonic discourse of the Middle East in the first half of the twentieth century, reached its apogee in the 1950s and 1960s with the rise in popularity of the Egyptian president, Gamal 'Abdel-Nasser. Pan-Arab organizations, including the Movement of Arab Nationalists (*Harakat al-Qawmiyyun al-'Arab*), were particularly attractive to many young Palestinians, who saw these groups as catalysts that would help liberate Palestine.

State control and oppressive living conditions (in the camps and elsewhere) also contributed to the lack of mobilization. It was as though Palestine was no longer a place or a people. Ian Lustick, writing of the first three decades of the emergence of

Israel, has argued that policies of segmentation, dependence and co-option[12] helped Israel succeed in controlling potential Palestinian political opposition. Similar policies were imposed in Jordan, Lebanon and Syria. To this day, fear of the direct consequences of open political activity remains a real concern for Palestinians living in these countries. In the newly established Israeli state, there was the additional fear related to campaigning for the right of refugee return, a far greater taboo in Israel than a call for equality even today. In some interviews conducted for this book, a few people would not speak to me for fear of repercussions and action by the states they lived in. One of my interviewees in the Wihdat Camp in Amman said 'Walls have ears' and another, who at that time had just arrived in Damascus from Nahr al-Bared camp in Lebanon in the summer of 2007, said that talking would lead only to more persecution and misery.

The potency of remembrance, which preserves what Rashid Khalidi calls the 'internal map'[13] of Palestine, is believed to be at the core of Palestinian refugee identity. Through remembering their lost land, such communities possess a rich, spontaneous, oral tradition that records the injustices and suffering of their past.[14] Following this logic, writes Diana Allan, 'nowhere is memory claimed to be – or rhetorically constructed to be – more authentic or vital than among refugees living in the camps.' Irrespective of their socio-economic background or whether they ended up as refugees, most of the people I spoke to about their lives and experiences in the 'lost years' spoke of pain and loss, or of suffering and survival. Some stories suggested that these traumatic experiences formed attitudes that eventually emerged to crucially change the social basis of Palestinian political power, deeply influencing the politics of subsequent decades. The *Nakba* was thus a period when a new generation of activists emerged – despite the Palestinians' extreme dispersion and fragmentation among the camps in Lebanon, Syria and Jordan, and inside Israel – managing to erase for a short time the class divisions that had plagued Palestinian society before 1948.[15]

In his memoirs, the Palestinian writer and activist Fawaz Turki, who grew up as a refugee in Burj al-Barajneh Camp in Beirut, writes:

> In our refugee camp in Beirut, my father complains that the Lord's way has become wanton and absurd, but adds that every event in His creation has reason, meaning. If it had not meaning, then what has happened to us would not have happened…. Maybe he was right…. I just know that for my own generation of Palestinians our last day in Palestine was the first day that we began to define our Palestinian identity. Like the olive trees and the land and the stone houses and the sea and the *dabke* dances and the ululation at weddings. Everything was where it belonged. Everything coalesced into a coherent whole. It never occurred to anyone to define it, or to endow it with any special attributes. Until we were severed from it.[16]

It is severance from the land that structured the experiences of the Palestinians whose stories I tell below. In their diverse locations, Palestine 'as a landscape' continues to loom as almost tangible, yet unreal – reproduced in the refugees' memory, a larger-than-life myth to their children – but it was the artificial and 'imposed arrangements of interrupted or confined spaces, the dislocations and unsynchronized rhythms of disturbed time'[17] that defined people's experiences in the years following the *Nakba*. It may be true that a homeland has no borders, but exile and dispossession do.

It is the experience of severance from their homeland that structures and permeates the eloquent narratives of Ellen Keettaneh Khouri, an upper-middle-class Christian Palestinian who lives in Beirut, and Abu Ma'an, who tells of his life in Hussein Camp in Amman and his struggle to overcome the difficulties of everyday life.

The subsequent stories point to the emergence of the Palestinian political subject and a new form of mass politics welling up from below among exiles and those in Israel. This comes across clearly in the remembered experiences of Khalil Jindawi, a Bedu forced to leave his encampment for exile in Yarmouk Camp in Damascus, and in the stories of Palestinians who remained in Israel. Hanna abu Hanna[18] was one of the first Palestinian intellectuals, writers and poets to break the silence inside Israel; Mohammed Ali Taha explains how his identification with his home town Mi'ar, which no longer exists, continues to define who he is. Finally, Ahmed Sa'adeh, a refugee in Damascus, tells how grassroots politics was transformed with the beginning of the Palestinian revolutionary movement and the idea of armed struggle, gripping the imagination of thousands of *jil al-thawra* ['the generation of the revolution'].

Nothing to hold on to but memory: Ellen Kettaneh Khouri[19]

I was born in Beirut in May 1948, which means I am an immediate product of my parents' exile from Palestine. I should have been born in Jerusalem. My parents had the baby room ready for my arrival, but they left in April and I was born in May. I think, or I am sure, that they left because my mother was pregnant.

There was no law or order in Jerusalem then and I wonder whether, had she not been pregnant, they would have stayed on. This is the beginning of my story and the beginning of this void, this melancholy, a mixture of *huzn* ['sadness'] and yearning that is not nostalgia. It is missing something you don't have, and maybe never had.

Our socio-economic situation was good compared to others, though my father comes from a humbler origin than my mother – she comes from a very wealthy, sophisticated, Westernized family. Her brother, for example, was the first person to drive a car in Jaffa, her home town. She attended a good school, and another of her brothers went to university, but all their wealth was, unfortunately, in their land and property, so 1948 and the loss of the land meant they lost their source of livelihood. It was a shock, because they had never imagined they would ever have to struggle.

My father, in contrast, was a self-made man whose parents died when he was very young. His mother was from Italian stock; her father came to Palestine and married locally. My father used to work for his wealthier cousins based in Beirut, but they all left for Lebanon during the 1948 war. He worked for them in Beirut after the *Nakba* since he left Palestine with hardly any money in his pocket and had lost all his life's belongings. When it became obvious they could not go back, he went off to Amman to establish a branch of the Kettaneh Company there. That's how we ended up in Jordan, in 1951, when I was two and a half years old.

I vividly remember the incongruity of my childhood. I had a mother who carried her family's social status with her into exile and who looked down on the backwater that was Amman at the time, and who would lament either the loss of Palestine or how her family went from riches to rags, though not exactly in that sequence or sense. I grew up with this bitter sadness, a mental beating of the worst type. I felt this void and anguish because of the loss of Palestine, and at the same time I had this sophisticated mother who tried to bring me up as different and superior to this backwater we found ourselves in. I rebelled against that, and that's one of my earliest recollections of what I would call being and feeling Palestinian, or what it means to be Palestinian.

It was a conflict that developed in different directions, but never was resolved. I felt I was cut off from a tree, as we say in Arabic: *ma'tou'a min shajarah*. Inside me was this burden, because I was constantly told that something called 'Palestine' had happened, and that is something that does not go away and something that you live. And you live with this and feel the dispossession, and feel cut off from the rest of the world and your larger family. I was cut off, too, from my immediate environment. In Amman, my mother brought me up in a way that made me feel I could be anyone growing up anywhere – in Paris, for example – but deep inside me I was somehow disconnected from anywhere. In fact, there was no question in my mind that I would never be anywhere where the presence of Palestine was not in me, and that what happened to Palestine was a very sad and unpleasant injustice that you had to basically intern- alize and absorb and live with every day.

But we did not talk about this, or at least I, as a child, would not talk about these feelings with my family or friends. In many respects, I had a normal childhood. I went to school, had friends, cried when I did not have a good grade and laughed when I did well. But in other respects, it was abnormal because my parents were the product of exile and they never forgot that. But they were not refugees. Their friends were the educated Palestinians, the elite society-in-exile that played bridge at the Philadelphia Hotel in downtown Amman, the place to go, to socialize and to swim.

That is what I remember of those days. I remember the war of 1956 [the attack on the Suez Canal] and how I pasted tape on the windows thinking this was a big deal and thinking that perhaps this would be the war that would change our fate as Palestinians. We listened to the news on the radio constantly. In fact, thinking about it, my life seems to be punctuated by continual war: there was the 1967 war, the 1970 civil war in Amman, the 1973 war, the Lebanese 1975–90 civil war, the 1982 Israeli invasion of Lebanon. Each felt as if it was a watershed, each time it hit me in one way or another and affected my movements.

At the end of the 1950s, we began to hear of the Palestinian Resistance Movement and, of course, of Gamal 'Abdel-Nasser. He used Palestine as a political slogan, but we followed his speeches avidly. Yet even as a child, it felt it was just another speech and that nothing was happening, or nothing would change. The early 1960s were my formative years when my political persona was formed and constructed. I thought of myself as an 'Arab nationalist social- ist', but I did not join any political party.

I went to a French boarding school in Jerusalem, Our Lady of Zion, between the ages of 11 and 18. Jerusalem was divided by the war, and my school was on the Via Dolorosa. It was so restrictive and the nuns were tough. Once a year, on the 15th of May, we were allowed to go out. Jerusalem would still be cold then and we would cover ourselves with blankets and wander onto the terrace to watch the fireworks staged to celebrate Israel's Independence Day.

We talked of Palestine all the time. I used to have arguments with my classmates about this, and we argued about who we were, about the right of everyone to have a home, about resisting and fighting back, and about the need not to accept that someone can take your land and get away with it. I became obsessed with news, more than anyone else I knew. I used to listen to news bulletins in the mornings and the evenings. My father owned this big radio with big knobs and I would turn to the BBC. I was so plugged in, and I used to think that if I were to be unplugged or to switch off, I would cease to be the same person: I would lose my identity.

I never regretted not joining a political group because I did not feel the need to be like everyone else. When I went to university in Beirut, I became aware of the existence of various Palestinian factions and heard of the first *fedayeen* ['freedom fighters']. I joined sit-ins and I went to help in the camps. In 1968, the student movements in Europe affected us and it was as if all my character came out then. I graduated in 1970. The situation was becoming worse and worse in Jordan. There was no question that my heart was with the resistance and, at the same time, I knew that things were coming to a head.

I had applied to go to London and I was accepted at the School of Oriental and African Studies. I wasn't at ease with my identity at that time. I loved London and I felt at home, because by that time I was sick and tired of being on the losing side of history; and, although I never denied my Palestinian-ness, I was ready to embrace another persona. That doesn't mean I stopped being a Palestinian, or being an angry person, but it was like me opening a window after being behind a closed door.

Now, I understand what went wrong. I felt dragged down by being part of a 'tragedy', by the *Nakba,* and I did not want to be dragged down any more. I had many identities, and I still do, but none of them is the right one, and none fits. What I told you is the beginning of my story; it is the early stage of what I am now, involved in the fields of human rights and democratization which was a natural consequence of my growing-up experiences and a desire to put part of the world right. What I have told you is not about mourning, nor about loss, but about the lack of something. It is about this melancholy and yearning that I feel. It is not nostalgia. It comes out on occasions, like when I watch the Olympics and I realize we don't have a national team, and when I remember.

I am more at ease with being Palestinian now, but being at ease does not mean it is no longer a problem. Being Palestinian is not stamped inside you, neither is it fixed, but it expresses itself as *huzn* that comes out of its hiding place and surprises you when you least think it would. It surprises me and fills me with sadness when I visit people in their homes and they tell me that they inherited this chest or that sofa from their grandparents or parents, and I suddenly realize that I have nothing to hold on to.

For me, everything started in 1948. I don't have anything else from my past. I don't even have my parents' marriage or birth certificates. To this day, I feel worried about buying a home because I don't know whether I will be squeezed out of my place and space. For Palestinians, nothing can be taken for granted.

Hussein Camp is my signature: Abu Ma'an[20]

I was three when I left Palestine, along with my two brothers, five sisters and parents, in 1948. We come from the village of al-Walajeh near Beit Jala on the West Bank, just 6 kilometres [4 miles] outside Jerusalem. I remember my father telling us that we left our village because of the Deir Yassin massacre. People were scared because we had heard that the Jews killed many people and raped women. And, for one reason or another, they were able to spread the news so that the stories became magnified, and we were terrified.

We stayed in Beit Jala for a couple of years, then came to Jordan, to Amman, because my father was a good farmer and was offered work by one of the large landowners at the time here. They gave him a piece of land between al-Juf and al-Taj,[21] and he grew cucumbers and bananas. I don't remember much about anything before that, apart from the stories I heard from my older brother and father about life before the *hijrah* ['migration']. They told me that when we left Beit Jala we only had blankets and a few coins, and they told me how we arrived in this area in Jordan called al-Salt, which was then empty, and how we built a tent out of rags and some other material. It was April and that year it snowed.

I don't remember the details, but in Amman we first lived in a cave, below a house owned by a man called Abu Khaled. He used the cave as a storeroom. We lived there and we used one of those blankets we brought with us for a door. When my father started to work, our situation improved – particularly because my older brother also found work as a waiter in a café called Qahwat al-Brazeel [the 'Brazil Café'] – and so we moved to the Hussein refugee camp in 1952. UNRWA [United Nations Relief and Works Agency] gave us what they called a *wihda* ['unit'] of about 100 sq. m [1,100 sq. ft]. These were actually tents of various sizes, depending on the size of each family.

The camp was muddy and wet, and winter was so harsh. I remember having to walk barefoot. It was a deprived childhood and, as children, we looked forward to feast days, when we would get extra food rations. If we were lucky, we would be given a shirt that often did not fit or a pair of trousers that might be too short. We played football in our spare time and often hit the ball against a rock or a piece of broken glass, and it would deflate. I loved school, even though a school then was typically a tent divided into classes according to age groups. It was noisy, though the teachers tried to keep calm and quiet. Then UNRWA began to build bigger schools, out of brick. Otherwise, we led very simple lives because we had no radio or television, but then my father bought a small German radio that was battery-operated in the 1960s. The other people in the camp thought we were rich and used to come to listen to the Lebanese singer Fayrouz singing nationalist songs.

At that time, people thought they were going back to Palestine. My father used to tell me that we would return after seven days, then it became seven months, then seven years. Now, it feels as if the tragedy has been going on for 700 years. Everybody talked only of Palestine. My father would talk to us about the land, how he married my mother, for whom he had to pay a handsome dowry in gold because she came from a wealthier background. We grew up with an imagined Palestine, a picture, no more, but it was a picture with an essence and a meaning, and a magical place to look forward to seeing and returning to.

I graduated from school in 1963/4 and, having excelled as a student, was given the opportunity to work in the Jordanian Central Bank as a clerk in the financial monitoring section. Life felt good for a while, because I enjoyed my work. Then the 1967 war happened. I remember when Jerusalem fell. It was late evening and we heard people outside shouting: 'They have occupied al-Quds.' My father broke down in tears. Can you imagine seeing that? We felt all hope was lost, and there is still no hope of getting back our homeland. When I say my prayers, I make one wish and that is to die in my homeland.

My father did not. I remember how hard he worked the land and how later on he went off to work in a brick factory. He would leave in the morning, carrying a small bag in which he had an onion, a tomato, some bread and a tin of sardines. When he returned, he would say his prayers and go to bed. Day after day, he would watch me studying at night under the light of a weak, solitary lamp. Each light bulb cost him half his earnings for a day, and he would say: 'Son, if you do not study, then you will have to work at the bricks.' I realized how important it was to learn, so I persevered and excelled in the national exam.

If you ask me, I would say that one of the best moments in my life was when I visited and lived in Palestine in the 1990s. It was such a wondrous feeling because nobody could tell me I was a foreigner. For the first time in my life, there was no one to tell me to get on with my lot in life or else go back to my homeland that was no more. In those days, I lived in Silwan near Jerusalem and those were the most liberating days in my life. I don't want to be romantic, but there is this smell in Palestine you cannot find anywhere. It is a smell that greets you at the borders when you cross the bridge and it fills you with warmth. I felt so free driving around the country, visiting Haifa, Tel Aviv and other places. I drove around during the day and sometimes at night just to satisfy this void, or hunger. I have no other name for it. The first time I visited Israel, I was boiling inside because I could not imagine this man, this stranger, living in my house, sleeping on my pillow, covered with my blankets.

I am well off, and my children are all doing well and successful, but I am still a refugee, with no homeland. I live on the outskirts of the camp now, but I imagine myself still in the camp. I shall never forget my camp years. In fact, look, this is my signature: *mukhayyam al-Hussein* ['Hussein Camp']. I can never forget.

Dheisheh Camp, Bethlehem: Um Basel[22]

I was called Hajar as a reminder of the *hijrah* ['migration'] – not that I needed reminding about our expulsion from our land, because I always heard stories of our homeland from my parents. They would tell me about the land, what plants they grew, how they lived and what they ate, so that the image of life there is so vivid in my mind.

My paternal grandmother would repeat the story of how a Moroccan man, an Arab Jew, told them they would leave their land one day and become refugees, and how she would not believe him because she could never have thought then that anyone would want to leave such a bountiful land out of choice.

They had apricot trees, their branches almost breaking with the weight of the fruit, and olive trees. They had a good life, not like us. These days you have to make an appointment to go visit your neighbour, just in case they're busy watching different soaps on television that they don't want to miss. In those days, people did not have any of these barriers and social demands: women would sit and drink tea and coffee together in the street, without television. Suddenly, they were reduced to refugees, begging for beans and rice, and flour and water from the United Nations.

They told me they had to leave when they heard stories of killings and rape, and reports of entire villages wiped out. One of our neighbours told us of the time a group of Jews came, and stabbed a man and butchered his pregnant wife. At the beginning, they thought they would be returning home, but then there was news of girls being kidnapped and raped in Deir Yassin and other places. They did not feel they had a choice. They left everything behind, my mother carrying my brother all the way on her shoulders because he was ill. They thought he was going to die and dug him a grave just in case. My poor mother!

I was raised here in Dheisheh Camp in Bethlehem. I went to school in the camp, then to Bethlehem for my secondary education. After that I attended a nursing college and worked as a nurse for 33 years. Our life was very hard at the beginning. I remember the tents that we lived in initially and the home that was provided for us by the UN agency. In fact, it feels as if my childhood was spent moving from tent to tent, carrying our possessions from place to place.

We had no heating during the winter, though we were given a *babour* ['stove'], which we could not use often because we needed the wood for the *kanoun* ['oven']. Ours was a big family, six boys and three girls, and we needed to keep warm, so all we could do then was close doors and windows, and sit close to my mother making tea and telling us stories. Each day before we went off to school, my mother would give us a cup of tea brewed on the *babour* and some home-baked bread. When we came home, we would find her cooking, simple dishes like lentils or aubergine stew. I was in secondary school when the 1967 war happened and Israel took over. Everyone was scared about what would happen to their women and daughters, mindful of what had happened in 1948.

But we remained in the camp and we are still here despite the Israeli incursions and attacks. It is like a big family and people look out for each other. I am lucky to have found Abu Bassel and married him. We are very happy together, thank God. We both worked and things were fine; it is just these last six years that we have suffered because of his health, when he had a stroke. Life goes on, but we suffered a lot over the years. But if you ask me, I would love to return to this paradise they keep telling us about, even if I were to live in a cave underground.

Homeland is to keep alive the memory: Khalil Jindawi[23]

I was born in the vicinity of Haifa in 1936 during the Arab Revolt. It might be possible I was born during the six-month strike that year, but we did not keep records, and nobody knows for sure.

All I remember of my childhood is that we lived in an area called al-Sa'idieh in the heart of the Carmel valley, close to Haifa. It was one of the most beautiful places on earth, with the water rushing from the mountains right through the valley into the sea. It was so pure we used to drink from it from our cupped hands. What can I tell you about my life then? *Ya Allah* ['Oh God'], it seems there is so much I remember, but little to tell when it comes to telling. Memory is so fickle.

As a boy, I worked as a *natour* ['guard'], helping my father, who looked after a factory, but we depended on the livestock, sheep, cows and goats, as other Bedouin do.[24] It is hard for me to think of the exact date when life changed, but the change came fast and with no real warning, though there were signs, such as the increase in the number of armed Jewish militias like the Haganah, a rise in armed attacks and a rise in the number of Jewish immigrants. Thinking of it now, they must have planned it for a while, because they wanted to make the area predominantly Jewish.

I remember this Jew, who spoke like us in good Arabic, and who befriended my father and spent a lot of time with him drinking coffee, as my father used to do. At the beginning, Abu Diab (this is what he called himself) would tell my father not to worry about the raids, but then these raids became more frequent and came out of the blue with no warning. With the increase in these attacks, sometimes there were two or three raids per week, we knew we had to leave. In fact, even Abu Diab told my father we had to, warning him that he could no longer offer him protection. That was why we left to join the *hamula* ['tribe'] in Shafa 'Amr at the end of 1947. I was 10 or 11 at that time.

Shafa 'Amr was so beautiful – even more than Carmel and Haifa – and fertile, with abundant water and trees. We set up our tents ['*buyout sha'r*'] near a Jewish settlement called Naharriya in a valley leading to the sea, and we stayed there until the *Nakba* – the defeat or whatever else you want to call it. There are no words to describe this tragedy. It was and is a catastrophe.

To this very moment, I remember the scenes of our departure and the overwhelming sense of fear. It was early morning when we started moving, and all I could see was this very wide valley which looked like a lake full of human beings. This lake was not only humans, but a mixture of various beings, animals, sheep, goats, dogs and donkeys, all walking together towards the north. Even for me, a child then, it felt like a tragedy.

I saw the battle between the forces of Shakib Wahab and the Jews. He was a Syrian Druze leader who watched the progress of the battle through his binoculars while sitting at the top of a tree smoking the *nargileh* ['hubble-bubble pipe']. I heard shooting from afar, and every now and then a donkey, carrying a couple of martyrs or some wounded people, would walk by *en route* to Shafa 'Amr where the ambulances were. We stayed in the Shafa 'Amr region for two nights and then moved on when it fell to the Jewish forces. Saffuriyyeh then was the next to fall, after some resistance by its inhabitants. We kept walking towards Kufr Manda till the morning. There is a valley there near Kufr Manda, named Abu Tur, which fell to the Jewish forces soon after Saffuriyyeh did.

Some people went back with their animals, but we did not, and it seemed that the decision to go to Syria was taken because we were worried our cows would not survive the cold. As it happened, most of our cows died on the way, and we were left with three, not enough to feed us any more. So we abandoned them and walked along with thousands of others. Sometimes, we would pitch our tents in random places and stay for a while, but eventually we arrived in Damascus, with no cattle or anything.

It was in Damascus that my journey of misery began. My brother and I did heavy manual labour to support my father, who by that time was too elderly to do much. Within two years, my older brother died and I was left to care for the family on my own. I worked in the fields and on building sites. I took on every possible job to make money because we needed clothes, food and furniture – I mean humble furniture, for some of the tents were just large enough to take a mattress and a straw rug to sit on. However, with time the situation in Yarmouk camp improved as UNRWA started to give each married Palestinian a piece of land of about 50 sq. m [550 sq. ft] so he could build a room and outbuildings for sanitation. Within a few years, the camp became a residential district, like any Palestinian one, but we did not forget the homeland. I got married at the age of 18.

When the attack against Egypt took place in 1956, I heard that the Syrian army was training a group of Palestinians for reconnaissance missions inside Israel. I decided to apply and joined the 68th Battalion along with several hundred Palestinian *maghawir* ['commandos'] under the command of Akram al-Safadi.[25] I served in the battalion for six and a half years, during which time I joined the Arab Socialist Movement, whose ideology I agreed with. I cannot say with certainty what triggered my strong Arab nationalist feelings, but it was probably the 1956 aggression against Egypt, and the fiery speeches of the Egyptian President Gamal 'Abdel-Nasser. I joined the movement because it was the only movement that could help us to free Palestine. With the breakup of the United Arab Republic,[26] our hopes – that a larger union, to include Iraq, Jordan and Lebanon, would emerge – were dashed. We believed so fervently in Arab unity and in Nasser's speeches broadcast on the radio or printed in circulars that arrived regularly, and for us the collapse of the union felt like an act of treason, and was followed by a real act of treason against us.

When secessionist officers seized power in Syria in 1961, they disarmed the *maghawir* and confined us to barracks. We went on strike, but they gathered us in a village called Beit Teemah in the Jabal al-Sheikh area and ordered us to go home. For me, this felt like the beginning of a conspiracy against the Palestinian people; we decided to join a group of pro-Nasser supporters.[27] They sent half of us to the Golan and the other half to Latakia, so we could not keep in contact with the other half. We went on strike, despite threats of execution by the-then Minister of Defence, and demanded that we be allowed to get back together as one group and return to our camp, which we had built ourselves, but they did not allow us to go back.

We decided to support the movement for re-unification, and carried out an attack to take over the radio station during the day. Most coup attempts, at least in those days, took place at night. We failed, so we threw down our weapons and prepared to escape. I hid in the attic at home and then escaped to my cousin's house. In the morning, a tank came roaring by and stopped outside. It was driven by an army officer, a Palestinian whose name was Mustapha 'Aradeh and who had a warrant for my arrest. I managed to escape into the fields where I met three of my colleagues. Encouraged by their company, we decided to head back to the camp, but as we drew close, we overheard a broadcast listing the names of our comrades, all of whom had been executed. All 18 *maghawir* were executed, and they mentioned our names as wanted criminals. We decided to escape. I went to Lebanon at the beginning, on my own, and then to Egypt, which offered us political asylum. I stayed there for 10 years, but I used to travel in secret to Jordan and Lebanon. I stayed until I was pardoned by the late Syrian president, Hafez al-Assad.[28]

If you ask me whether I would do this again, take up arms to fight and risk my life, I will tell you yes, even now at the age of 72. Every time I see a group of children throwing stones at an Israeli tank, I realize our people did not die for nothing. There are people who hang pictures of Palestine to remind them of their homeland. I don't need to be reminded. I get overwhelmed with a mixture of emotions, but without these memories, I would have died a long time ago, like a withered old tree that has no use any more. My life would have ended.[29]

April 1948 was the cruellest of months: Hanna abu Hanna[30]

Hanna abu Hanna was born in the village of Yibna near Nazareth in 1928. He founded several cultural magazines, was a dedicated educator and has published 21 books of poetry, narratives and scholarship, as well as 15 books for children. I met him in Haifa.

I am one of three children. I spent my childhood moving around Palestine, spending time in Jerusalem, Ramallah, Haifa and Nazareth because of my father's work. I began getting involved in politics, protesting against British rule, as a student.

I was eight years old when the Arab Revolt started, and I remember reading the pamphlets about joining and getting enthusiastic about it. For me, the revolt was the start of what I call the Palestinian wound. I was studying at the Arab College in Jerusalem. Up to then, only a handful of students joined protests because of the threats of expulsion, but we were charged up and enthusiastic. My teachers were so important in forming my political being. Many of them were communists.

My life was transformed in 1948, like all Palestinians. Two years before, I remember walking along Jaffa Road in Jerusalem with some schoolmates. On the walls, there were huge posters in Hebrew and Arabic, promising the Arabs treatment as citizens with equal rights in what was then talked of as the Jewish state. It was the beginning of our dilemma and the transformation of a majority into subordinate citizens. The events that followed two years later shook me profoundly. We were not fully aware what partition meant, though we had plenty of speeches to listen to. And we were some of the elite few, who considered themselves informed. It is history now. But even before the British left, the coastal towns, such as Haifa and Bisan, had been taken by the Jews. With no real Palestinian leadership, we were powerless in the face of the Zionist plans to expel us all.

When I heard that Abdel-Qader al-Husseini had died a martyr in the battle of al-Qastel, I was shattered because it was the beginning of a series of defeats. And then we began to hear news of various massacres, at Deir Yassin and Nasser Eddine, a village near Tiberias, before hearing of the fall of Jaffa, Haifa and Safad. My friend Saliba told me that we had no choice but to accept the

UN resolution because partition was better than losing all. He was arrested along with seven other members of *Jaysh al-Inqadh* [the Arab Liberation Army] and charged with treason for having voiced his opinion and supported partition. April 1948 was the cruellest of months. There were battles almost every day.

We did not give up. Even when Israel was created a month later, we were not daunted, but began a campaign to form organizations and societies to mobilize our youth. We set up the Youth League in Nazareth and Haifa, and began to establish branches in the villages. I was a teacher of Arabic in those days, so I had access to young people. I joined the Communist Party because I believed in its mission and ideology. Later on, it would begin talks with Israeli communists to give the minority Palestinians more voice. Some people (those outside Palestine) accused us of being collaborators. It was only through the work of the assassinated Palestinian writer Ghassan Kanafani that people understood and appreciated what we were doing.

Military rule between 1948 and 1966 was harsh and we needed permits to move around. Spying and collaborating with the Israelis became a normal thing, because the Israeli intelligence apparatus and their spying agencies were lethal, and managed to infiltrate the masses and interfere with our personal lives. I was about to get engaged to a fellow teacher, but I was threatened and told I would lose my job if we got married. Can you imagine? I asked her to decide.

We, the Palestinians who stayed behind, were cut off from the rest of the Arab world and forgotten, but there was Gamal 'Abdel-Nasser to listen to and to remind us of our Arabness and our role in the larger Arab community. He was so much loved and revered among Palestinians inside Israel that streets would empty whenever he was giving a speech. There was one occasion when I was walking along a street in Nazareth when he was talking and I could hear every word he said through the radios turned on to full volume and which I could listen to through the open windows in each house. I did not miss one thread in his speech even though I was out walking.

Resistance in diverse forms, such as cultural production, meant we were able to survive. In 1953, I founded the journal *al-Ghad* ['Tomorrow']. We published poems, short stories and other forms of literary work with a message of defiance and resistance. We were the first to publish Mahmoud Darwish. We held memorial services for the martyrs of Deir Yassin, called strikes and asked people to come and listen to us read the poetry of resistance. During my youth, we felt that our future was also the future of our people and that struggle would reap rewards. And all along, we knew we would not bow to pressure to abandon the land.

In 1959, I was asked to help establish a new school. The director was a well-educated young man who had received a master's degree in Britain. The Communist Party would not allow me to help, but when it became short of funds, I was given approval. This school became the Orthodox School in Haifa. I started a campaign to find teachers with the same ideological thinking and nationalist feelings. It was a pioneering school that produced some of our best scholars. People doubted that we could succeed in the face of Israeli government pressure and restrictions, but we did. We did not have books sometimes, but we had great minds.

Do you think military rule has ended? Even today, they can arrest you at any time, on grounds of posing a threat to state security. I was arrested in 1956 on those grounds and kept in detention for three months. I have written about this in my three-volume memoir – a story of survival and existence under the British who protected the Jews, the revolutionaries, about my life as a teacher under occupation and now as an Israeli citizen.

Surviving the *Nakba*: Mohammed Ali Taha[31]

That June, I remember standing watching the Israeli troops approaching at sunset, shooting indiscriminately at the villagers still busy in the fields collecting their crops.[32] When they had finished shooting, they began destroying the houses. I knew my village Mi'ar was no more.[33]

I was born in either in 1941 or 1942. I cannot remember the exact day and I don't have the documents because my father left the birth certificate, along with other official papers, in an iron box in our house in the village. When we were able to return after the occupation, we could not find the box. Perhaps they thought there was money in it. My mother says that I was born in either March or April. I remember our village well, and the children I played with, though I have not seen some of my friends since 1948. Some have gone off to Lebanon, others to Syria and some to the Gulf. Some died in exile.

Our village, Mi'ar, was very beautiful because of its position and altitude. When the Jews came, we left, along with the extended family, for Lebanon, but my father changed his mind when we reached the border and decided to return. So we went to Sahknin to the east of Mi'ar, on the day the truce came into effect. We stayed there for 18 months before moving to the village of Kabul south of Nazareth. I never forget Mi'ar. Though most of the houses have been bulldozed, I still remember where my house was, where the fig tree was, where the water came from. I took my sons there and I still take my grand-children to visit. It has changed: a club stands on the playground where I played as a child, but I can clearly see my house, no longer there, with the pomegranate tree. As a child, I used to look at Mount Carmel from my window and hear the sea beyond. My relationship with Mi'ar is so intimate that it is quite difficult to convey in words, but I have been writing about this since 1960 in different forms and ways.

I have published about 35 books for children, and the most tender stories are about 1948, the tragedy. I cannot forget this because I lost the house, the fig tree, the well and, most importantly, I lost friendships I made as a child. Most of my friends are not here. We are peasants, but we had the land, and in the course of one day we had nothing. It was the olive-picking season when we left, and my mother carried some olives in a shawl arranged over her head. They started to fall as she began walking briskly, away from danger, and my father stopped to collect them. But as he did, even more fell out. He was a religious man, and, in despair, he looked up at the sky and shouted: 'Oh God, the country is gone, the village is gone, the possessions all gone, what do You want of us more than this?'

I cannot tell you exactly when we, as Palestinian young men and women inside Israel, began to develop nationalist feelings or when we started to struggle against the Israeli occupation. In the immediate aftermath of the *Nakba*, we just struggled to survive. We were lucky not to have become refugees, but the Israeli military rulers did not leave us alone. In 1951, 1952 and 1953, they would come, lay siege to our homes and areas, and gather women and men in one place, then they would load all those with no identity cards onto trucks and take them to the Jenin area to be deported.

In those days, it was dangerous to mention the word Palestine. In schools, anyone who said Palestine would be kicked out. They intervened in everything, in every detail of our daily lives. There were no libraries, no intellectuals left, and most of the people were peasants who could not read or write. The nearest Arab city to remain almost intact was Nazareth; others, such as Ramleh, Lydd, Jaffa and Haifa, were destroyed. But in the midst of all this, and despite it, a new form of politics began to emerge, in underground writings and poems, and in schools. The Communist Party began publishing a newspaper, *al-Ittihad*, and soon people began to talk about the rights of the Palestinian people. I was a fan, and it was through reading this paper that I began to hear and learn about Palestinian literature and the great writers and thinkers before 1948, poets like Ibrahim Touqan, Rahim Mahmoud and Khalil al-Sakakini.

We began to write ourselves, starting a literary resistance movement that stirred nationalist fervour and anti-occupation feelings. We called this 'the literature of resistance'. I wrote a story called 'The hour' about a clock in Nablus that stopped at 12:00, but, when Palestinian youths turned out to throw stones at the occupation forces, the clock would start again; and I wrote another story about a camp under occupation. I was imprisoned for my work. At school, my best friend was Mahmoud Darwish. We sat side by side on the same bench. He got a distinction in maths, but I was better at Hebrew. We started to write our poetry at the age of 15. My first story – called

'When will my father return?' – is about a child whose father goes to battle in 1948 to fight the Jews, but does not return. The child continues to wait for him.

I can say now that Israel is a democratic state for Jews, but we, the Palestinian Arabs, can only enjoy the crumbs of this faulty democracy. For 18 years, we had no democracy or centre to turn to and we were subject to military rule. We were banned from speaking and put under house arrest. Each word we scribbled had to be passed by the military censors. When I taught, I was always under surveillance, watched for any utterance on anything related to my being Palestinian. In 1968, I was accused of burning the Israeli flag on Israel's Independence Day. It was a made-up story, meant to terrorize me and find an accusation against me. I was not fazed.

The Palestinian national movement began here, in Israel. When the refugees outside Israel were talking of return, we, the people inside, were battling for our survival, because we knew from our own experience that the Zionist project aimed to empty the land of its people. They used to come here to Kabul, besiege the place and gather men and women in one place and then deport those who did not have an identity card. We began to build bridges with the Palestinians in the West Bank and Gaza, and through them with the rest of the Arab world. The election of Tawfik Zayyad as Mayor of Nazareth made a huge and palpable difference, as did the election of Bassam al-Shak'a in Nablus.[34] Both are nationalist leaders who worked under occupation.

They [the Israelis] imposed emergency rule at the end of the military administration, which meant that the Minister of Defence could restrict our freedom. Many people were banned from speaking out and all stories had to be passed by the censor. Then they cancelled the emergency rules, but oppression remained.

I became more active in 1983, following the Israeli invasion of Lebanon, making public speeches and writing more. It was then that I wrote several books, one about a girl from the Dheisheh refugee camp in Bethlehem, and another on the meaning of flags. I could not find a single literary journal willing to publish it [the latter] until I gave to the journal *al-Ittihad*, which was then edited by Emile Habibi, and it was published in London.

I was warned that I could be imprisoned and, one day, the Israeli police came and confiscated all my books and took me to Acre Prison. They accused me of sympathizing with what they called a terrorist organization, the PLO. You could get a seven-year prison term. I was released later on, but it took nine months to drop the accusations against me. They did not stop chasing and harassing me. I thought it would be easier to teach at the Orthodox College in Haifa, but I was deluded. They threatened the school with closure and tried to fire me. I have told my children my story and I now tell it to their grandchildren, so the story does not get forgotten.

The gun was my bride to cherish: Amad Sa'adeh'[35]

I was born in one of the districts of Ramallah, 'Ayn Siniya, in 1949. I spent my early childhood in the Jalazone Camp near Ramallah, but we [my family] are originally from the village of Salmeh near Jaffa, the last city to surrender.

Many of the villagers went to 'Ayn Siniya after the *Nakba*. When conditions worsened, we moved to Jalazone Camp, and then to Amman. My father worked as a teacher in Madaba in Jordan. I remember clearly those early days as refugees, the structure of the camp, the tents. I tried to locate our tent the other day when I came across some pictures of the camp in its early stages, but I could not find it.

I went to a school in the al-Ashrafiyya area in Amman, at the height of the Algerian struggle for independence, and I remember singing the Algerian national anthem at school. We were not allowed to mention Palestine by name, so Algeria, the symbol of resistance to colonial rule, was the next best thing. One incident remains vivid in my mind. I was revising in class and the teacher came to check my notebook because I had made a mistake. And he asked me: 'Where are you from?' and I replied: 'Palestine.' I did not know what would happen. He beat me with a cane and asked

2 One of UNRWA's first priorities in 1950 was to set up schools for refugee children, on rocky hillsides, in tents and in rented premises. Jalazone Camp in the West Bank 1951. Photograph: UNRWA.

me to stand facing the wall. Then he asked me the question again and, each time I answered that I was from Palestine, he beat me even harder. I realized it was taboo to mention the word 'Palestine'. I was ten at the time.

My mother died when we were still in Jalazone Camp. To this day, I find it painful to talk about this, but she never adjusted to life in the camp. My memories about my time there are of a miserable existence. There were the tents that would fall over when a strong wind blew. And there was the bitter cold. One night it snowed and I thought I would die from the cold. There are other memories, of my father telling us about his life before 1948 and about the time he joined the 1936–9 Arab revolt. He, too, found it hard to become a refugee and decided he wanted to teach, even though it was for a meagre salary.

For me, the word 'Palestine' is associated with pain and suffering, and being Palestinian means being the 'other', the 'alien'. Our Arab friends made us feel different. We had to be kept apart. Sixty years on, we remain exploited and marginalized. You pay a heavy price for being Palestinian. Just look what is happening these days; the news of continual suffering and violence.

My parents did not want us to be involved in politics or in any political activity, so we had to become activists in secret. I did not even know that my three brothers had also secretly decided to join the resistance, and I only found this out when we all ended up in the same prison in 1970. We three had joined different Palestinian factions, but that's another story. I joined Fatah in 1967, in Lebanon, just before the 1967 war.

We were fired up and there was this whole generation of Palestinians, 16 to 17 years old, who grew up in the camps, in misery, exile and alienation. We wanted to be different and do something. I was not yet 16 when I was arrested for the first time, by the Jordanians. I had taken part in a protest against the Israeli storming of the village of Samou', but the Jordanians did not want any agitation at the time. It was this background that made me search for an anchor and an identity. We were so fired up with nationalism, particularly after listening to the speeches of Nasser on *Sawt al-'Arab* ['Voice of the Arab'] radio station and the station's fiery rhetoric. Of course, this rhetoric let us down in the 1967 war.

We had not heard much about Fatah until we heard that it had launched a military operation in Gaza.[36] It was an operation that restored our hope and belief. I, along with some of my student friends at school, thought we could form an armed faction on our own and do the same, carry out an operation in Israel. We held meetings, had heated debates about ideology, about honour and dignity, about the land and the meaning of Palestine. But we did not have the money to buy even one gun. And, all the time, there was this organization Fatah awaiting us.

I was not a political animal, not interested in positions or ideologies, like many others of my age. I wanted to be given a gun and to go and fight the enemy. Of course, it was romantic; the revolution was a romance, something to fall in love with. I remember listening endlessly to this song, based on a poem by Mahmoud Darwish, *Rita wa al-Bunduqiya* ['Rita and the gun']. And I knew the gun was a bride to take and to cherish for life. It was what I wanted.

Notes

1. Most of the Bedouin population of the Negev, which had not been included in a census since 1922 when it numbered about 65,000, was expelled in successive waves after 1948. For more details see Rosemary Sayigh (1979/2007) *The Palestinians: From Peasants to Revolutionaries*, London: Zed Books.
2. Yezid Sayigh (1997) *Armed Struggle and the Search for State: The Palestinian National Movement, 1949–1993*, Oxford: Oxford University Press.
3. Fouzi El-Asmar (1975) *To be an Arab in Israel*, London: Frances Pinter Ltd, p. 5.
4. The only exception was when Egypt was embarrassed by Israel's 1955 raid on Gaza, which led Egypt to briefly allow operations by Palestinians inside Israel.
5. For more details on citizenship status and political rights, see Sayigh, *Armed Struggle and the Search for State*.
6. Ibid., p. 41.
7. Ibid., p. 46.
8. Rashid Khalidi (2006) *The Iron Cage*, Oxford: Oneworld Publications, p. 135.
9. Ghada Karmi (2002) *In Search of Fatima: A Palestinian Story*, London: Verso, p. 210. Karmi notes how nobody in England seemed to remember Palestine and how in the 1950s the name itself quickly went out of general use.
10. It was during this period that Golda Meir made her infamous remark: 'There is no such thing as the Palestinian people.... They never existed' (*Sunday Times*, 15 June 1969).
11. Rashid Khalidi (1997) *Palestinian Identity: The Construction of Modern National Consciousness*, New York: Columbia University Press.
12. Ian Lustick (1980) *Arabs in the Jewish State: Israel's Control of a National Minority*, Austin/London: University of Texas Press.
13. Khalidi (2006) *The Iron Cage*, p. 205. Rosemary Sayigh also refers to this phenomenon: "The village – with its special arrangements

of house and orchards, its open meeting places, its burial ground, its collective identity – was built into the personality of each individual villager to a degree that made separation like an obliteration of self"; see Sayigh (1979/2007) *The Palestinians*, p. 107.

14. Diana Allan (2007) 'The politics of witness: remembering and forgetting 1948 in Shatila Camp' in Sa'di and Abu-Lughod (eds) *Nakba: Palestine, 1948, and the Claims of Memory*, New York: Columbia University Press.

15. Khalidi (2006) *The Iron Cage*, p. 137.

16. Fawaz Turki (1988) *Soul in Exile*, New York: Monthly View Press, pp. 17–18.

17. Said (1986) *After the Last Sky: Palestinian Lives*, London: Vintage Books, p. 20.

18. Others who broke the silence included such authors as Ghassan Kanafani, Ez-eddin al-Manasra and Mo'in Bseiso in exile, and Mahmoud Darwish, Tawfik Zayyad and Samih al-Qassem in Palestine.

19. Ellen Kettaneh Khouri (2008). Personal interview with the author, Beirut: August.

20. Abu Ma'an (2008). Personal interview with the author, Amman: August. Abu Ma'an is now a successful businessman. His full name is Mohammed el-Aydi, but prefers to be known as Abu Ma'an.

21. Al-Juf and al-Taj are two of the seven hills that Amman was originally built on.

22. Um Basel (2007). Personal interview with the author, Dheisheh Camp/Bethlehem: April.

23. Khalil Jindawi (2007). Personal interview with author, Yarmouk Camp/Damascus: August. Khalil Jindawi sadly died in 2008, a few months after speaking to me. He began his life as an illiterate Bedu living on the outskirts of Haifa and ended it a poet, teacher and writer.

24. The Bedouin identified with the grasslands on which their livestock grew and fed. They had a strong sense of loyalty to families and clans, but were said to enter into alliances with almost any force offering them material and political benefits. The image of Bedouin warriors, wild and noble, dominated both the Orientalist literature and general Western perceptions of Palestinian society.

25. Yezid Sayigh writes that the *maghawir* were under strict orders to avoid combat in Israel, but Syrian military intelligence used

them for covert operations against domestic and Arab foes. See
Sayigh, *Armed Struggle and the Search for State*, p. 67.

26. Egypt and Syria formed a union in 1958.

27. Jindawi was not clear about the sequence of events, but – according to Yezid Sayigh (1997) *Armed Struggle and the Search for State* –
Safadi, who had been transferred to Cairo during the union with
Egypt, had secretly recruited several dozen Palestinian fighters
and then slipped into Syria secretly to lead an assault on army
headquarters on 18 July 1963.

28. Yezid Sayigh, in *Armed Struggle and the Search for State* (1997),
says that the Syrian authorities, confronted by the strength of
pro-Nasser sentiment, set up new security units to observe political activities among Palestinian refugees. One of these was a
Palestinian detachment [*al-Mafraza al-Filistiniyya*] made up of
former 68th Battalion personnel and entrusted with active surveillance and policing, while another was the 'Palestinian section' [*al-Qism al-Filistini*] attached to the Ministry of the Interior.
The Syrian experience demonstrated the potential dangers of
Arab sponsorship of Palestinian military formations.

29. Jindawi died a few months after the interview.

30. Hanna abu Hanna (2007). Personal interview with the author,
Haifa: November.

31. During the period of Israeli military rule (1948–66), there was
negligible study of the Palestinians remaining in Israel, which
maintained tight control over all forms of political expression
among its Palestinian minority. Under military government
rules, the Palestinian community was classified as being in a
transitional stage – a traditional 'primitive' Arab minority in the
process of becoming modern citizens. Israel was considered to
be a democratic state. See Sabri Jiryis (1968) *The Arabs in Israel,
1948–1966*, Beirut: Institute for Palestine Studies, a detailed
account of life under military rule (first published in Hebrew in
1966, and updated a decade later), which was the first widely read
work to break out of the mould and detail Israeli restrictions on
Palestinian movement and other discriminatory policies.

32. Forty people were killed in the shooting spree, part of the few
thousand Palestinians who perished in the attacks and massacres that accompanied the ethnic cleansing operation; see
Pappé (2006) *Ethnic Cleansing*. Mi'ar was one of the first villages to fall prey to this strategy that the Israeli troops used.
This strategy started with summary executions to speed up the
expulsion. On the site of what was Mi'ar, there are several Jewish

settlements – Segev, Yaad and Manof – built in the 1970s, after Israel confiscated the land under its plan to Judaize and de-Arabize the Galilee.

33. Mohammed Ali Taha (2007). Personal interview with the author, Kabul/Nazareth vicinity: November.
34. I tell Shak'a's story in Chapter Four. Tawfik Zayyad's wife also tells her story in that chapter.
35. Ahmed Sa'adeh (2008). Personal interview with the author, Damascus: April.
36. For details, see Chapter Four.

CHAPTER THREE

Raising the *Fedayeen*: Between Romance and Tragedy, 1964–70

Between Rita and my eyes there is a rifle
And whoever knows Rita kneels and prays
To the divinity in those honey-coloured eyes
And I kissed Rita
When she was young
And I remember how she approached
And how my arm covered the loveliest of hair-braids
And I remember Rita
The way a sparrow remembers its stream.
Ah, Rita!

Between us there are a million sparrows and images
And many a rendezvous
Fired at by a rifle
Rita's name was a feast in my mouth
Rita's body was a wedding in my blood
And I was lost in Rita for two years
And for two years she slept on my arm
And we made promises
Over the most beautiful of cups
And we burned in the wine of our lips
And we were born again.
Ah, Rita!

What before this rifle could have turned my eyes from yours
Except for a nap or two, or honey-coloured clouds?
Once upon a time
Oh, the silence of dusk
In the morning my moon migrated to a far place
Towards those honey-coloured eyes
And the city swept away all the singers
And Rita
Between Rita and my eyes – A rifle

(Mahmoud Darwish)[1]

It was a little over a decade after the *Nakba* that a small group of Palestinians, led by Yasser Arafat, met discreetly in a home in Kuwait to work out the organizational structures of the Palestinian resistance group Fatah (the reverse acronym for *Harakat al-Tahrir al-Filastini*) or the movement for the liberation of Palestine, thus beginning a new chapter in Palestinian politics.

The young leaders of Fatah, including Arafat's would-be senior aides, Salah Khalaf and Khalil al-Wazir, went on to galvanize the masses with their militant rhetoric forcing a major change in the social basis of political power that would deeply influence the politics of subsequent decades.[2] Donning military fatigues and the Palestinian *kuffiyeh* – instead of a suit and a red *tarbush* – the leaders of Fatah[3] radically changed the way Palestinians were represented, bringing to the fore a new generation and a new image. The new revolutionary leaders were drawn from diverse class, social, religious and regional backgrounds. Significantly, many of them had lower-middle-class, rural or refugee-camp origins.[4]

Yasser Arafat,[5] who headed Fatah, the Palestine Liberation Organization and the Palestinian Authority, began his political activities in Cairo in 1952 when he was elected president of the Palestinian Student Union. Along with his trusted colleague Salah Khalaf (who under the name of Abu Iyad was Arafat's chief aide-de-camp until his assassination in 1991), he fashioned a radical agenda for the Palestinian people. In his memoirs, Khalaf later wrote that the leaders of Fatah were convinced that the Palestinians needed to rely on themselves and should not expect anything from the Arab regimes.[6]

Fatah began as an underground cell, promoting its vision and ideology through a monthly magazine called *Filastinuna* ['Our Palestine'] that began publishing in Beirut in 1959. Soon, Fatah began recruiting and training cadres, creating hundreds of cells in border areas with Israel, and also in Palestinian communities in the Arab world, Europe and America. The group planned its first military operation against Israel for 31 December 1964 when commando units from the West Bank, Gaza and Lebanon were to cross over into Israel to attack military and economic targets, but their attempt was foiled.

The ultimate goal of Fatah in the 1960s was plain: to liberate the whole of Palestine and remove Israel as an economic, political and military entity. In this respect, it did not differ from other Palestinian groups that had also begun to take shape. One of the more prominent ones was the Arab Nationalist Movement [*Harakat al-Qawmiyyun al-'Arab*], which coalesced in 1951 around a group of students at the American University of Beirut, fronted by George Habash, the son of a relatively wealthy Christian trader from Lydd, and Hani al-Hindi, the son of a respected Damascene family.[7]

In the mid-1960s, the group changed its name to the Popular Front for the Liberation of Palestine (PFLP); its main goal was liberating Palestine, but it considered this would not be achieved unless the Arab countries were free from Western control. Another key faction at this time was the Democratic Front for the Liberation of Palestine (DFLP), led by Nayef Hawatmeh. Some Palestinians also joined pan-Arab and transnational groups, including the Ba'ath Party, the Muslim Brotherhood, Islamic Jihad,[8] the Syrian Socialist Nationalist Party and the Arab Nationalist Movement.

The Six-Day War – *al-Naksa*

By the 1967 Six-Day War, which ended with Israel's occupation of the West Bank and Gaza Strip, many of the smaller groups had amalgamated with Fatah.[9] The war, dubbed *al-Naksa* ['the setback'], marked a watershed in Palestinian history because it tipped the balance of power in favour of the guerrilla organizations of the Palestinian Resistance Movement and away from the thus far elitist establishment of the Palestine Liberation Organization.

The 1967 war also changed the balance of power among the Arab countries that were defeated – the Arab republics of Egypt, Syria and Iraq, and monarchic Jordan – creating a regional power vacuum and giving the Palestinian guerrilla groups the opportunity to forge ahead, independent of Arab control. As a result of the war and the extension of Israel's control over Palestinian lands, the Palestinians once again were divided into new geopolitical categories. Communities in the West Bank, the Gaza Strip and within Israel itself were for the first time since 1948 united by the sheer fact that all were under Israel's control. All had to come to terms with Israeli rule.[10] From the very outset of its occupation, Israel declared the new areas as 'territories under custody' in which military rule would apply. Any form of resistance was brutally quelled, and new regulations gave the army the power to expel anyone suspected of being a security risk. In fact, in the decade after 1967, the Israeli military frequently destroyed houses, expelled people and arrested Palestinians without trial, acts that came to be known as collective punishments.

Attempts by the Palestinian Resistance Movement to establish underground cells and bases in the occupied West Bank and to launch guerrilla attacks from within the territories largely failed, but resistance to Israel's occupation was more significant in the Gaza Strip until at least 1972. During that period, religion assumed a more important role in some people's lives. At first, people were attracted to the Egyptian-born Muslim Brotherhood, but then turned to Palestinian organizations such as Hamas and Islamic Jihad, which had emerged with a clear national-religious agenda.[11]

The camps in Lebanon, Syria, Jordan and the occupied territories were swollen by a new wave of displaced people, the *naziheen* of 1967 (as opposed to the *laje'een,* the 'refugees' of 1948), the thousands of people fleeing or expelled by force from the territories newly occupied by Israel. However, this new wave resulted in a smaller demographic shift than in 1948. In 1972, 1.5 million refugees were registered, of whom 650,000 lived in 13 large refugee camps in Palestine, Jordan, Syria and Lebanon.[12] Gradually, many of the refugees gravitated towards the Palestinian resistance movement. Hundreds joined, particularly following the dramatic rise in border attacks against Israel. In Jordan, the number of recruits more than doubled within three months of the Karameh battle,[13] which was a key catalyst for the revolutionary guerrilla organizations to move their action above ground, take off politically, and redefine the nature and tactics of the Palestinian–Israeli conflict.

The PLO,[14] led by Arafat and his Fatah faction, now became the main political institution that attracted Palestinians, directed them and shaped their consciousness. Although the PLO managed to create broad zones of autonomy and independence only in Lebanon, its efforts there, as elsewhere, led to disastrous conflict – perhaps none worse than the war with Jordan in 1970, which the Palestinians called Black September. A year earlier, Palestinian groups had begun setting up training camps and bases in south Lebanon and Beirut and forming alliances with various popular Lebanese factions that agreed on opposition to Israel's role in the area. The first guerrilla bases, set up in south Lebanon in 1968–9, began to launch attacks against Israeli settlements in the Galilee soon after.

The PLO's control went far beyond the Palestinian camps and the guerrillas had nearly free rein in a wide swath of Lebanese territory, including the coastal cities of Tyre and Sidon. In the context of deteriorating relations among Lebanon's confessional groups, the ensuing tensions helped generate one of the bloodiest conflicts of the twentieth century, the Lebanese Civil War of 1975–90, which brought yet more disasters and acts of brutality. Lebanon ended up facing two Israeli invasions – a limited incursion in 1978 and a full-scale invasion in 1982.

Romance of the revolution: the myth of the *fedayee*

Various dates are given for the beginning of what has become known as the Palestinian Revolution [*al-thawra al-Filistiniya*]. Some give the date as 1 January 1965, when Fatah announced its first military operations inside Israel; others suggest 21 March 1968 when the Battle of Karameh[15] took place.

What is beyond doubt is that the call to armed struggle arose directly from the historical experience of the Palestinian people,[16] increasing in strength and power with the expansion of education and Palestinian political consciousness. Young workers, students and refugees in the camps, like Samira Salah, Salah Mir'i, Mohammed Naguib Mahmoud and Laila Khaled, whose stories/part-histories I tell below, became some of the first *fedayeen*, while middle-class Palestinians like Walid Salim al-Taybi took up white-collar forms of struggle: organization, diplomacy and information.[17] Like others who joined the resistance movement in the early 1960s, he speaks of those days as the best in his life:

> We were fired up with nationalism. The homeland was our ultimate goal. Fatah managed to infiltrate the masses. I decided to join. I did not have a political position and at first I just distributed flyers and leaflets detailing plans for struggle. I was delegated to set up an archive, putting together cuttings and stories in Israeli papers dealing with Palestine. I spent hours doing that. I was a foot soldier, too, though I never became a *fedayee*.[18]

The *fedayee* ['one who sacrifices himself'] would be portrayed in pictures and posters with head wrapped in the Palestinian *kuffiyeh*, gripping a Kalashnikov,[19] an image that drew on visual memories of the *mujahideen* who rebelled against the British and their Zionist protégés during the revolt of 1936–9. By the end of the 1960s, the *fedayee* had come to dominate Palestinian symbolic politics, becoming the centre of a constructed heroic national narrative of steadfastness, struggle and resistance. Armed struggle became the central element of the 'imagined community' of the Palestinians.

With the adoption of armed struggle as the primary, almost sole, means of national resistance in the 1960s and 1970s, militants began to commemorate 'battles' in visual artefacts and ceremonies. Throughout the years of *al-thawra* ['the revolution', 1969–82] in Lebanon and elsewhere, photographs of guerrillas in battle focused on heroic markers: young and virile men, sometimes with the shoulder-length hair fashionable at the time, laughingly preparing to enter conflict. Palestinian cinema in that period acquired the name 'cinema of the Palestinian revolution', embracing its causes and ideas.[20] Armed battles were considered a virtue, as they transformed passive refugees into active fighters, and, as some leftist political organizations claimed, subverted social hierarchies so that 'traditional' Palestinians became 'modern' by taking up arms.

This subversion of tradition informs the stories in this chapter, particularly that of Samira Salah and her years as an activist and Laila Khaled's account of how she became involved in the PFLP hijackings of airliners. Laila defied her traditional background, in the process becoming an icon of resistance and a role model for many young Palestinian women. Laila, along with a comrade from the PFLP, hijacked TWA Flight 840 on its way from Rome to Athens on 29 August 1969, diverting it to Damascus. No one was injured, but the aircraft was blown up after the hostages were asked to disembark. On 6 September 1970, she attempted another hijacking, this time of an El Al flight from Amsterdam to New York, as one of a series of hijackings carried out by the PFLP. The attempt was foiled and the flight diverted to London, where Laila was held for about 45 days until her release as part of a prisoner exchange.

Laila became a national and international household name in 1970s, her large, dark, doleful eyes peering from under a *kuffiyeh* covering her hair, her arm holding a Kalashnikov, with the Palestinian flag close to her chest. Posters with this image adorned homes and public spaces at the time, and still do. Laila remains politically active as president of the PFLP's women's branch and as a member of the Palestine National Council. She now lives in Amman, Jordan, where I met her in August 2008.

Next is Mohammed Naguib Mahmoud, who told his story with much emotion and nostalgia. Indeed, many of the *fedayeen* I interviewed, whose accounts I could not include, broke down in tears when they recalled the pride, the sense of purpose and the meaning of resistance in their revolutionary years, sweeping aside or intentionally ignoring the fact that involvement in battles might also have caused suffering and loss. In all these interviews about memories of *al-thawra,* the themes that emerged of their common fate, camaraderie and rituals, bringing the guerrillas together as a Palestinian imagined community that viewed armed resistance as its *raison d'être.*

In these narratives, courage and sacrifice in the face of death are central elements of the mystique and romance of being a revolutionary fighter, but there is also humanity, tenderness and vulnerability – sentiments and experiences that are missing in official Palestinian narratives of great heroism and struggle. The tenderness and vulnerability of the young, inexperienced, yet totally committed *fedayee* comes across most evocatively in Salah Mohammed's account, the last in this chapter, when he talks of his capture by the Israelis at the beginning of the invasion of Lebanon in 1982. He was a mere child at the time, and he reverted to being a child as he sat in his cell or in his hospital bed in Israel crying out for his mother.

I also include some stories of life under occupation in the West Bank and Gaza in the first years after their occupation in the 1967 war. The first is by Samia Nasser Khoury, a middle- to upper-class Christian Palestinian who tells of the occupation in an East Jerusalem suburb and elsewhere. The second is by Issa Ahmed Issawi, living in the village of Issawiyeh, close to Jerusalem, and the last is the story of activist-cum-artist Zuhdi Alawi, who grew up in the Gaza Strip.

These last two include prison experiences that offer a vision of prison as a place of dynamic resistance, growth and learning. Like other personal narratives in this chapter, the prison stories[21] are constructed through a complex interaction between individuals and the diverse existing narratives to which they have access.[22] Issawi and Zuhdi use discourses of empowerment, not victimization, when talking about their time in prison, showing how it can serve as a school or university, and as a space in which the 'imagined community' of resistance and political agency emerges, despite Israeli oppression.

A life in halves: Laila Khaled[23]

I was born in 1944 in Haifa. I don't remember much about life there, though the image of the stairs in our house and the banisters come to my mind whenever I hear explosions or gunfire. Maybe this is because my mother used to ask me to hold on to the banisters when I came down the stairs whenever a gun battle erupted in the vicinity.

On the day we left our home, my mother told us we were going to Lebanon and, as she called us to assemble, she began to count heads. I did not come down immediately. Noticing I was not there with the others, she shouted at me: 'Why don't you answer, Laila?' At that exact moment, a shell hit the car. I told my mother later that I did not answer her immediately because I wanted to

3   Laila Khaled in her house in Amman holding a picture of herself as the famous hijacker. Photograph: Tanya Habjouqa.

take all the dates in the kitchen so that the Jews would not get them. Thinking we were going for a short break, I took a box of powder for my baby sister. My mother cried all the way, and we cried along with her.

My parents are originally from the Lebanese city of Tyre, which we used to visit every summer. The road from Haifa to Tyre is not long and takes about an hour by car. When we arrived there from Haifa, we went straight to my uncle's house. My father stayed behind to fight, along with some other revolutionaries. He was later arrested by the Egyptians in Gaza. It was April and the citrus and orange trees at my uncle's house were bearing fruit. I reached out to pick an orange only to have my mother slap me on the hand. 'These are not for us. Our oranges are in Haifa,' she said. It was from that moment on that I began to hate oranges. My mother always talked about what was ours and what was not, what we lost, what we could not have and so on, so the idea that we could never own a house or anything else until we returned to Haifa was planted firmly in my mind.

Life went on and we were soon at school. The first school I went to was a tent, literally, with a class in each corner. It had a makeshift board. We used to sit on the sand because there were no benches. I did not like it at all and told my mother I did not want to go to school, but she took me to one side and said: 'Look out of the window and look at the camp. Look, you are no different, despite the fact you live in a house, so you go to the same school.' My mother was adamant we have a good education and would cut the pencil in half with a knife and give each child a piece of it. We got half a sheet of paper to write on, and it seemed everything was in half. In 1960, my father had a stroke and lost his memory, but he remembered the past and he would always repeat 'The land has gone and so have the children.' I often wonder what he meant.

I am the sixth child in a family of 12. When I finished school, I was told I should find work. But I insisted on going to university, and it was through sheer determination that I applied to the American University in Beirut without telling anyone and was accepted. I had no money to pay for the fees so I went to meet the dean of students and tell her my story. She thought I was joking, but I told her my brother, who was working in Kuwait then, would support me. I also told her I wanted to study agriculture, a subject reserved for men, because I wanted to help plant our land once it was liberated. We were so romantic in those days.

It was at university that I started to be openly involved in political activism and I was, after all, in the company of George Habash and Wadi' Haddad, who were to become the public face of the PFLP. Unfortunately, I did not finish the degree because I could not sustain myself financially and was forced to go to Kuwait to teach, at the beginning of 1963. I remember telling my mother that I would either come back as a guerrilla fighter or in a coffin. And she would insist that only when no more men are left, the door would be open for women to take on different roles.

My father was more liberal in his thinking and in his behaviour. Though we grew up in a conservative society, he did not force us to wear the veil. Of course, women were subjugated in many ways, and I am sure this has something to do with how characters form. Though I did not like what she said, I was secretly in awe of my mother, who was single-handedly able to look after and control 12 children when my father was no longer healthy and could not do much. But I did not listen to her talk and started training in the use of arms, in Jordan. When I finished training, I was asked to carry arms across the border to Beirut. I remember the border guard asking me why I was travelling late at night and I told him it was not his business.

And so it was in the middle of the night that I arrived at the house of Wadi' Haddad.[24] He sat me in the kitchen and asked me whether I was ready to die, and I answered: 'Of course.' Then he asked if I was ready to be arrested and I said: 'I am not better than anyone else.' Then he asked me whether I could hijack a plane, and I said I could not imagine what that involved. It was a time when the *fedayeen* were beginning to be known and when women were also becoming martyrs. I was personally inspired by Shadia abu Ghazaleh, who was my age when she was martyred, and by 'Aysheh 'Odeh and Rasmiyeh 'Odeh, who both went to prison in Israel. The Algerian revolution against the French was taking place and had given us much hope that we could resist the colonialists too.

My dream was to carry out an operation inside Palestine, but I felt this option [aircraft hijack] would be good enough, for the time being. I was well briefed and prepared. I knew the operation would attract world media attention and raise questions about who the Palestinians are. The flight we were planning to hijack was going from New York to Tel Aviv, via Rome and Athens.

I boarded in Rome, where a man sat beside me on the bus that took us to the aircraft. He told me he was Greek and that he was going to visit his mother in Athens. I became absent-minded, because I remembered an incident that keeps haunting me. It was perhaps in 1963 or 1964, when my father was allowed to visit the Mendelbaum Gate, the former checkpoint between the Israeli and Jordanian sectors of Jerusalem, north of the western edge of the Old City along the Green Line, to say hello to his mother whom he hadn't seen since he left the country. When he returned after seeing her, he became ill, and became paralysed and unable to talk.

Anyway, as agreed with the PFLP leaders, I went to the first-class cabin and the man, the co-hijacker, went to the economy class. After half an hour in the air, we asked people to raise their hands, I brandishing a revolver in one hand and holding a grenade in the other. I did not intend to use them. I then announced that we were PFLP guerrilla fighters and requested the pilot to take us to Tel Aviv. I then read out several messages to inform the passengers of our plans and why we were doing this. Suddenly, as we approached the city, and the coastline of Palestine appeared, we heard that Israel had sent two military planes to intercept us. We had to divert to Damascus, where we let the passengers out and gave ourselves up. We were held for 45 days, during which time a prisoner exchange took place. It was worth it to make our cause public.

Men cry, too: Mohammad Naguib Mahmoud[25]

When I arrived at Burj al-Barajneh Camp in Beirut on a hot August day, the electricity was cut off, and the air was thick with heat and dust in the small schoolroom where I had arranged to meet Mohammad Naguib Mahmoud, a *fedayee* turned artist-cum-teacher. He was in a wheelchair, as both his legs were amputated following a serious injury during the Camp Wars (1985–8).

I was born in 1952 in south Lebanon. I was about two years old when I realized we really did not have anything, because my father did not work. The Lebanese people in the south treated us well and I have no problems with that, but we had to move to Ba'albek, then Beirut, then Nahr el-Bared, then al-Rashidiyah, then Burj al-Barajneh, where I have been since I was four.

We had a radio that we listened to sometimes, but I would mostly sit around listening to the women talking about Palestine and how wonderful life was before the *Nakba*. The comparison with our conditions then was so stark and painful, and I questioned what had happened and why.

I used to go to school barefoot. My mother never put away clothes, but just piled them in a corner as though ready to go on a trip. 'We must keep them this way, because we are returning to Palestine tomorrow,' she would repeatedly tell us. So my brother and I grew up with this idea and hope of imminent return. My father, who fought with the *mujahideen*, would tell us stories about the blond, blue- or green-eyed European Jews who came and lived nearby, and settled in houses, and of the fights that later ensued. We grew up dreaming of this mythical place, abundant with pro-duce: figs, watermelon, grain, flour, eggs and olives.

And then one day, when I was about 11 or 12, I saw this amazing sight. There was a group of *fedayeen* parading through the narrow streets, wearing all their battle gear, their faces cov-ered with *kuffiyehs* and their arms high above their heads, hold-ing their guns high in the air. I knew that I wanted to be one of them. Some of my friends felt the same way and we decided to go to the PLO representative in the Mazra'a area in Beirut to tell him about our plans. We did not have shoes, but we walked there. The Fatah leaders took one look at us and told us to go back to our camp to study first, but the idea of joining the would-be liberators of the homeland did not go away and we began to talk more about it.

It was the 1967 defeat that made us even more determined. We had heard about training camps in the Shtoura and Jdeidah areas in east Lebanon, so we went there, again walking. We were about 25 young men – teenagers, really. When we got there, a guard stopped us, asking what we wanted, and we told him that we were Palestinians from the camp and that we wanted to become *feday-een*. He sent us to a man called Abu Ali Iyad and we repeated our demands, and he warned us that training was tough and that we needed to learn how to jump through burning tyres and walk on glass, but we were convinced and managed to impress him. They accepted us for an 18-month training period.

I will never forget how I felt when I went back to the camp, wearing my outfit and carrying my gun. My mother ran along the street ahead of me, telling everyone that her son was a *fedayee*. It brings tears to my eyes because when I was training, I would write and tell my mother not to cry for me. And she did not. It was a magical feeling. Everybody loves a *fedayee*; the girls, the boys and the elderly adore you, but this is innocent and deep, a love that feels pure. If you told someone you wanted to marry their daughter, they would give her to you without asking. I would walk in my uniform round the camp streets, and people would stop me to touch me, just as they would the garb of a religious man. The memory makes me cry[26] – because of the lost hope, and that energy and the feeling that I am doing something. I am doing something now, but my life is nothing in comparison.

In 1969, we got into some trouble with the Lebanese army. I cannot remember the exact reasons for that, but they came in at night and shot my maternal uncle and somebody else from the Ayyub family. We decided to take over the camp. We, the young men, stood guard at the gates and everybody stood with us. We took part in some operations against the Israelis, setting up traps in the south and infiltrating the borders in northern Israel. Every time I went, my mother would ask me to bring back some soil, so I would bring a pocketful of soil to her in my pocket and she would put it in a different bottle each time. In those days, we all worked together, Fatah, the PFLP and the DFLP, but it was the Arabs who made us fight each other and make concessions.

I joined the revolution to liberate Palestine, but then we found ourselves involved in the Lebanese Civil War. It was something we could not control – though, thinking of it now, we did make some mistakes about alliances. I fought in the battle of Tal-al-Za'tar in 1976, and that was a savage attack. The Lebanese Amal fighters who attacked the camps in the camp wars (1985–8) nicknamed me *Iblis* ['Satan'] because I was a good fighter and would not allow any of them in.

It is sad to talk about this phase. I am imprisoned here. I cannot leave the camp because I am a wanted man, having killed many of our

4 A Palestinian refugee woman, who identified herself as Um Khaled, and her family at Al-Bas camp in Tyre in Lebanon. They are displaced Palestinians from Nahr al-Bared camp following the 2007 battle between the Lebanese army and the Islamist militant group Fatah al-Islam which killed more than 400 people and displaced up to 30,000 Palestinians. Um Khaled feels bitter about her life, but life goes on. Photograph: Tanya Habjouqa.

opponents myself. I have put away my gun now. I am done with fighting. I paint to express my feelings and to tell the world I exist. Paintings can speak and act for you, and they bring hope to the children of the camps. They are as good as guns.

Women are not mere hyphens: Samira Salah[27]

I was born in Tiberias in 1944, but we lived in Haifa because my father was working in the city. I was one of 11 children, four of them boys. We left in 1948 for Irbid in Jordan, and then continued on to Damascus. I always wanted to find out what was going on, so I followed the news on the radio avidly, and my parents talked to us about Palestine and politics all the time.

I gave my first public speech in 1956, on the aggression against Egypt. I was only in the fourth grade, but I was encouraged by my teacher, a Syrian with strong pan-Arab nationalist views. I volunteered to talk, and that was the beginning of my political activism. When Gamal 'Abdel-Nasser visited Syria in 1958, I went with a group of my classmates to greet him outside the Republican Palace. We put on special clothes to show we were Palestinians, and I wore a hat with the word 'Palestine' sewn across the top. We elbowed our way to stand close to the balcony where he was standing, and someone took a picture of us with him in the background. I still have that picture.

I joined the students' union and then the women's union because I felt we women were oppressed. We continue to see this oppression to this day everywhere, in homes and outside. I owe my determination to my mother's generation, too, because they were the silent, hard workers who brought us up. My parents married young. It was an arranged marriage, but they were very fond of each other. My mother used to smuggle my father pistols to use in the struggle against the Jewish militias in Palestine, despite the fact she could have been imprisoned by the British for collaborating. My father, who became a member of the Arab Nationalist Movement, was imprisoned many times.

In 1963, I joined the Arab Nationalist Movement. It was then that I met Salah, my husband-to-be. I then became a member of the Popular Front for the Liberation of Palestine, whose vision matched mine. I got married in 1970 and then came to Lebanon, and all the while I was involved in different organizational activities related to the liberation movement and to the women's union.

The 1967 war was an unforgettable experience. At that time, I was in Saudi Arabia working as a teacher in al-Khobar. I enjoyed that time because I had the opportunity to learn about other Arabs, outside my own community. When the war broke out and we lost, my Saudi friends were so concerned and worried about the expansion of Israel. It is hard to describe my feelings at the time, but I felt that liberating Palestine might have been a dream after all. I decided to leave my job because I could not bear being so far away from everyone, and because the homeland was becoming an image or a dream.

I moved to 'Ain el-Hilweh refugee camp in the south of Lebanon when I first married Salah. He was asked to go to Jordan when clashes broke out between Palestinian guerrillas and the Jordanian army. Oh, those were years of successive failures, and the collapse of the Palestinian resistance in Amman [in 1970] was heart-breaking.

Here in Lebanon, we ended up taking part in the civil war amid rising tension and fears that we, the Palestinians, were on the road to being annihilated. No revolution could have been successful under those conditions, but we were at fault, too. We paraded the streets carrying our arms and in our full armoury, and felt we were in control of the south of Lebanon. We carried out a few incursions and operations against Israel, but the Lebanese Civil War finished us off. I remember living through this war, the battles, the guns, the bits of shrapnel falling all around. I had two children and I was pregnant with the third.

It is a myth to say women were left behind and were not part of the revolution. We were not mere hyphens. We were active, at home and on the battlefield, tending to people who had lost martyrs, relatives or who were displaced. During the month of Ramadan, we distributed food to the fighters on guard at different intersections and front lines. So the experience was that of unity and solidarity. We were one in those days, man and woman. But we did not know what was happening, nor did we have any idea about the magnitude of the Israeli invasion of 1982. It finished off the idea of struggle, and the peace camp won. We stayed put in the camp despite the hardships, because we were determined not to run away as we did in 1948. And despite the loss of innocent lives, we were hopeful and things were possible. *Now, we have no more hope.*

In those days, we were encouraged to ask questions, told to write down our concerns and discuss them during meetings. It was not necessary for us to carry weapons to fight, though we received military training and we could do it. We used to take shifts, stand guard at night, so that the day fighters, the men, could rest. I manned the entrance to the camp at night and cooked food in the day. That period was so important for women and activism.

Now you see this excessive veiling and retreat of women. I keep telling young girls not to marry early, as they do, because they will not be able to teach their children anything. I speak to women and tell them stories about our role in the struggle and ask them to stand up for their rights. Staying at home is not good enough, but the battle to win their minds and hearts is tough with the rise of the Islamist trend.

When I came to 'Ain el-Hilweh as a young bride in 1970, I was considered an outsider and people would say I was not a real refugee. But I soon made friends and began to feel the camp was my home. It is different in the camp. It is a community. I still go to 'Ain al-Hilweh every day, even though I live here in West Beirut. In 1982, Israel tried to break down this feeling of community and tear people apart, as they have succeeded in doing in Palestine, but they could not do that. In the camp, there are these young people who never saw Palestine, but they still want to fight for it. Golda Meir was once quoted as saying: 'The old will die and the young will forget.' She is absolutely wrong. The old will die and the young will *not* forget.

The honeymoon did not last: Samia Nasser Khoury[28]

I visited Samia Nasser Khoury at her home at a top of a hill in Beit Hanina.[29] She was born in Jaffa in 1933 to a well-to-do family and brought up in Ramleh.

I remember my grandfather's home in Jaffa. We used to visit it a lot, but it is Birzeit – even in those pre-*Nakba* years – that I remember most. We were really lucky compared to others, because we could move from one place to another with little difficulty and because our financial situation was good. I remember swimming in the Dead Sea in the middle of the night with the moon shining down on the water and I remember how I learned to swim in Lake Tiberias, such a beautiful lake.

I don't remember much of the years after the *Nakba*. They were uneventful, and nothing seemed to be going on, but I do remember hearing of the Arab Nationalist Socialist Movement and Arab unity. For us ordinary people, life seemed to fall into a pattern. We were under Jordanian rule and allowed to move about with no restrictions. Life in Ramallah, where I was living at the time, was very pleasant: we socialized, went to parties and generally got on with our lives. We used to go to Cinema Dunya to watch movies, mainly Egyptian films at the time.

I worked with my father in his office at Birzeit College (that is what it was then) between 1954 and 1960, the year I got married. Those were some of the happiest times in my life. I married Yousef, my late husband, out of love, after going out with him for two years before that, so we knew each other well before committing ourselves. I have four lovely children. It is so tough for our children now, with all these restrictions and these checkpoints that drive me mad with anger.

In 1948, we were living in West Jerusalem, staying in rented accommodation, so our departure was not as harrowing as it was for my uncle, who owned his house and lost it. There are, of course, Palestinians who had to leave under the threat of the gun. We did not have to, but it was fear that something might happen to us that made us go. We had heard of the massacres and the killings, and we were scared. I was 14 at the time. Even then in those early days, we were convinced we would return. We could not believe that Israel had any intention of changing the face of Jerusalem.

Even in 1967, when they occupied us, we were not so certain about their intentions for Jerusalem. Suddenly, these new houses went up and Israel's policies soon became clear:[30] The year 1967 was a big defeat. We were just about to celebrate our fourth wedding anniversary, in this house I am speaking to you in. We were also planning the wedding of my nephew. The day before, we visited the church where he was to get married. For some reason, it was full of Jordanian soldiers.

On the wedding day, there was no trace of them. My sister was planning to come over from Rome, but she called to say she was worried because there had been talk of war breaking out. The wedding went ahead, but the streets were empty and an eerie silence had taken hold. We were preoccupied and did not pay much attention to news, until my father called to tell me to bring the children over to Birzeit for safety. He had heard of a possible attack or war breaking out and he was worried because we had a Jordanian army outpost on the hilltop just outside our house.

I panicked. Without thinking, I gathered all the photographs of my children, and then my children. At the back of my mind was the memory of 1948 and of those people who told of lost family goods, never to be retrieved. You can buy new furniture and find work, but you can never get back photos. Yousef said he would stay behind because he did not want to leave the house unoccupied. As I left, I wondered whether we would ever go back. I stayed with the children at Birzeit College with my father. It was safer to be there than in the larger towns and cities which were coming under attack. On the fourth day of the war, a small van drove along the street. Someone, speaking through a loudspeaker, told people to raise white flags and surrender. A woman shouted across the street that the Jordanian army had withdrawn the night before.

In reality, it was not a six-day war, more like 24 or 48 hours. Within two days, Israeli soldiers were walking around with no resistance and not a single bullet to frighten them off. Had we been armed in the Old City of Jerusalem, things would not have been so easy for them. I cannot tell you how we felt. It was a mixture of deep sadness, disappointment, resentment and bitterness. The occupation of Jerusalem was a real tragedy, the ultimate tragedy, and remains so to this day.

Yousef called to say that two Jordanian soldiers tried to put up a fight against the invading forces, giving the impression that more than two men were defending the outpost. After a couple of days, he took pity on them and went out to give them coffee, but by that time they had given up and were getting ready to flee. In Birzeit, we were not spared. The Israelis entered houses and occupied the dormitory. We told them we had no water or electricity, but they did not seem to mind. We wondered when they would leave, and they did so on a moonless night [*fi laila ma fiha daw 'amar*]. But we knew we were under occupation.

And suddenly in the midst of all this defeat, we began to talk and dream about seeing our homes in Jaffa and Haifa. The Green Line was no longer divisive. The people of Galilee were the first to come and visit, and warned us that the 'honeymoon' period with Israel would not last. They told us of their own occupation, of the land confiscations and of the detention of innocent people. In fact, when we did visit, we saw with our own eyes how oppressive Israel had been. Only a handful of houses had been left untouched, unchanged. The 'honeymoon' did not last.

Soon, we began to feel the effect of our occupation. They began to impose some incredibly restrictive rules, taxes, and began to exploit Palestinian workers. They conducted a census and started issuing special identity cards for Jerusalem residents, and then annexed Jerusalem illegally. Any act of resistance[31] or opposition to the new regime was met with force. My nephew Kamal was one of the first people to be deported because of his nationalist views. In their attempts to squeeze us, they would not give you this permit or that if you did not co-operate and follow their rules.

In those days, it was really tough to be a mother or a teacher, trying to keep the spirits of the young generation high. You could not work out how to adjust your values, what to tell your children, what to teach or what to say, when even mentioning the word 'Palestine' was considered taboo. We, as Palestinian women, had to be involved. With men jailed, women were needed to help support families.

We suffered as a family because of these controls, though our socio-economic situation was very good compared to others. My brother Hanna, the founder and first president of Birzeit University, was deported in 1974 and remained in exile for the next 19 years.[32] My son was jailed because he composed a piece of music about the 1987 *intifada*. He made a mistake by going to record his work in Israel, because we have no studios here, and they arrested him and imprisoned him for six months. It was difficult to visit, but you draw some strength when you see other parents, mothers in particular, waiting to see their children, with heavier sentences and harsher conditions awaiting them inside and outside. You try to draw on your faith, but you realize how religion and belief have been exploited to approve oppression. And then you reach new levels of distress and hopelessness when you realize that nothing can be done.

I went to Birzeit College at the age of 17. I studied business administration. Though he encouraged me, my father did not want me to study abroad. I worked briefly with him, but since my marriage in 1960, I have worked as a volunteer because my husband was able to support the family financially. I was the headmistress of the *Rawdat al-Zuhour*, a primary school here in Jerusalem. I was so happy because I felt I was educating the new generation. Now the young generation is frustrated and people are losing hope. You just have to go to Salah-al-Din Street in the Old City and see these youngsters not doing much, just smoking *hashish*. Then you have these checkpoints that you deal with every day. I could not arrange a memorial service for Yousef because of people having to negotiate the checkpoints.

Then you have the Palestinian divisions, and you see red flags, green flags and yellow flags raised in these protests, and people forget they are dealing with a ferocious enemy and that they must stick together.[33] It makes me angry, but you learn to be calmer when you grow older. This is what it means to be Palestinian, to care, because if you stop caring, then you let go. We cannot let go. I shall keep trying. There is a need to keep talking and telling our story, even though it might be like a lone voice in the wilderness. This is the only way to communicate our continuing story.

I did not waste my life in prison: Hani Ahmad Issawi[34]

I remember 1967 very well. For us, it was not a real war. It began with artillery firing. We were in our houses, because there were no bunkers to hide in. In three days, the war ended and we were occupied. There was no resistance. They came in jeeps, and they gathered men and asked those who had weapons to disarm. They imposed curfews, but would allow people to go work in the fields, because it was harvest time, between six in the morning and three in the afternoon.

The confrontations with the occupation forces started early. I was then in the final two years at school, and the first confrontation with the Israelis was over the content of the curriculum. They wanted to talk of Jerusalem as being part of Israel, and wanted to include historical references about Israel since its creation in 1948. These were, of course, flawed and told the narrative from their point of view. The Israelis had their plans already in place and appointed new teachers to replace those who went on strike in protest. Some of these teachers were Palestinians from *al-dakhil* ['the interior' or inside Israel]. This confrontation took place in 1968, coinciding with the Karameh battle. I was a student at the Rashidiyyah School in Jerusalem, and it felt as if this confrontation was the first national action, which began a new phase in my life.

Occupation means a new reality and new experiences. Along with strikes and protests, we felt a need for public resistance in different ways. At that time, we were influenced by pan-Arabism, by the images of the *fedayeen* and their operations. We knew some of the guerrilla leaders – who were working here underground – by name, and met some of them, too. People treated them like mythical figures and heroes. All the while, the occupation was tightening its grip, and the phase of demolishing houses, a much publicized and severe Israeli practice against us, began. The first house to be demolished was that of Salah al-Namiri, whom they accused of taking part in a military operation.

I would firmly say the nature of politics and resistance changed in March 1968. It became grassroots and popular, rather than top-down and elitist. Ordinary people, and not heroes or mythical figures, took part in acts of resistance and protest. I was one of the masses, taking part in the first wave of protests against the changes in the curriculum. In those days, the image of Israel was one of a mighty country that was invincible, but after the

Karameh[35] battle, our views and feelings changed and we felt that we could fight back and face the enemy. I joined the underground resistance in 1969 and started planning a military operation. In the meantime, we were contesting, through protests, everyday acts of violence – the demolition of houses and confiscation of land, in a farming region where people depended on agriculture for their basic needs.

It did not make a difference which party you joined, or which party did more than the others, because what mattered then was to act and mobilize. We did not care whether it was Fatah or Hamas, or DFLP or PFLP, though the most active organizations at that time were Fatah and the PFLP. Here, in the Jerusalem area, the PFLP had a visible presence because it had help from supporters of the Arab Socialist Movement, which had been active in the Jerusalem area, people like Daoud and Ishaq Maragheh, and others. Fatah, however, moved fast to mobilize people after the battle of Karameh and many people joined it.

We did not carry out our operation. I was arrested in September 1970, just after the civil war in Jordan [Black September]. It might have been an informant. Of course, I was arrested many times after that, but that first period in prison was the longest behind bars, ten years. I was accused of belonging to a 'terrorist' organization and possessing weapons. Somehow, those ten years did not feel long, though by any standards spending ten years in prison is long. Prison life[36] was hard because the Israelis were intent on making us confess and breaking our spirit. Torture was brutal, and we were treated like prisoners of war.

The prison near Sarafand, Armon ha-Avadon (known as the Palace of Hell), had the reputation of being a slaughterhouse.[37] There I spent my time in solitary confinement. They gave us an hour of freedom a day, and were allowed to walk in the prison yard, in pairs. But it was half an hour walking and half an hour sitting. When I first went to prison, I really did not think the occupation would last all those ten years, and we were hopeful that a solution would be found. We managed to survive by organizing ourselves and making sure we continued to read and learn.

They used torture techniques, physical and psychological, when they wanted to extract information. Two of our fellow prisoners died because of ill health after they were tortured. One of the techniques they used when we went on hunger strike was to push a pipe down one's throat to push some salty liquid in. We heard them screaming with pain. Often, the only thing you heard was crying and screaming. I myself was sent to hospital after going on hunger strike for 33 days. I was later sent to Ramleh Prison where I began to study and I learned Hebrew. I did not feel I had wasted ten years of my life.

Imagining rainbows: Zuhdi Hamoudeh al-'Adawi[38]

My parents are originally from Lydd in Palestine, but they left for Gaza in 1948 as refugees. The situation in Gaza has always been bad, worse than anywhere else. Those members of our extended family who went to Jordan, for example, had better chances and a better life.

I was born in Nusayrat Camp, known as the middle camp, in 1954. We lived like other refugees, poor and destitute, under Egyptian administration – but we were not allowed to visit Egypt. Our parents, like most other families in the camps, never stopped talking about their homes and towns in Palestine, so I grew up with this idea of return or of doing something to retrieve what was taken by force. They also talked to us about the Israeli invasion of the Gaza Strip and the Sinai Peninsula in 1956, which initiated the Suez War. As a child, I had this image of the Israelis as inhuman people, and more like scary owls that attack at night.

In those days, a small unit of the Arab Liberation Army was stationed in Gaza, but under the control of the Egyptians. This unit left its weapons behind after the defeat in 1967. There was no resistance, though some of the older people in the camp tried to fight back. It was during those early years of the occupation that a young man called Samir Hassan approached me and suggested I join the Popular Front for the Liberation of Palestine. He was not that much older than me. The idea of being a resistance fighter attracted me, and I began to have visions of myself running around with a gun and attacking the occupiers. I agreed.

I was perhaps 15 or 16 at the time, but I looked older because I was tall and broad shouldered, because I used to play sports. In Gaza, there is a popular saying along the lines that Gaza belongs to the occupation in the daytime and to the resistance at night. This is not a figment of the imagination, because I experienced this myself during training. In fact, there were times when we would walk about at night and did not see any Israeli soldier, though we did see their jeeps in the distance.

Military training, all in secret, took no time and neither did it take time for the Israelis to capture us on our first real foray. Someone must have informed on me or I would not have been captured. I was a child, a teenager, and it felt surreal to be interrogated by those huge men in uniform and experts in extracting secrets. I was arrested in April 1970 and taken to a prison in Gaza where I, along with others, was held for nine months before being sentenced to life imprisonment. When the Red Cross visited us, and we had the chance to ask how long a life sentence was, the answer was 99 years. Can you imagine how that felt for a child of 16?

Life in the early days in prison was hard because the Israelis were so clever at damaging people and draining them, leaving them empty and useless. We somehow managed to keep our spirits high in those early days by talking about the struggle. I was taken to Askelon Prison where I met older people – teachers, engineers and university graduates – as well as ordinary people like myself.

And it was there that I first experienced being a student. Prison turned into my private university. We used to have small meetings whenever possible, with someone giving us a lesson on some topic. We started asking for books and were allowed some novels, nothing intellectual or political. We resorted to cunning techniques, asking our families to bring us books with the covers replaced by covers of stories and novels. We started learning more. We learned Hebrew, too.

We were kept in small rooms, perhaps six to seven metres [20–23 ft] in length. They gave us a radio that could only receive Israeli radio broadcasts. We would listen to the news in the morning and evening, and then we would sometimes be allowed to listen to some songs by Um Kulthum [an Egyptian singer]. Soon we were allowed Hebrew newspapers, such as *Yediot Ahranot*, which we used to read voraciously. For me personally, prison was an important stage in my life, which influenced all that came afterwards.

In my childhood, I painted as a hobby, and drew portraits of famous people. In prison, I did not have the material to draw on, so I used pillow cases and pieces of cloth torn off sheets to draw on. I would cut each pillow case into four pieces and draw a picture, a landscape, anything that I could think of or imagine. You need imagination in prison, to survive. I used to imagine myself on the beach in Gaza. My family managed to smuggle in some coloured pencils and brushes, which they wrapped inside cigarette paper. I was caught doing this within a week and, when they questioned me about the missing pillow case and I could not provide any answer, I was put in solitary confinement for one week. In those days, the word 'Palestine' or anything to do with Palestine was a crime. And all my paintings were about Palestine and resistance.

In prison, the struggle continues, but it is not the struggle of carrying a gun. It is the struggle of the storyteller, the painter, the politician and the leader. When the Israelis incarcerated us, they thought we would come out broken, like rotten tomatoes, but we came out apples. The prison is not defined by its walls, but by the relations inside it. They close the gates and you see only iron, no green, white or blue. The plates we eat from are the colour of death, yellow, and the clothes we are given to wear are red. But we were able to imagine the colours of the rainbow.

I was released in 1985 and came to Syria because it was the only country that would accept Palestinian prisoners of war.[39] I have since been painting and earning my keep as the arts director at *al-Hadaf* magazine, the publication of the PFLP. The other day, we asked some children in Gaza to send us their artwork. One of them sent us a picture with the words: 'Please, let us sleep.' It reminded me of my prison days.

The RPJ kid:[40] Salah Mohammed[41]

I am a child of exile. My great-grandfather was related to 'Abd al-Qadir al-Jaza'iri, and they lived in the Magharbeh district of Jerusalem – or this is the story I heard from my parents. They come from the village of Ma'bar near Tiberias. I was born in Yarmouk Camp in Damascus in 1968.

My parents would talk of Palestine as though it was this huge country, or a Paradise, that had everything you could think of. They would tell us about the goodness of life, about their riches, about their customs and about how happy they were. They were the products of *al-Nakba* and I am the product of *al-thawra*.

I never had a childhood. Although I went to school, I began training with Fatah at the age of five. At 13, an older friend told me he was going to Lebanon to fight in the south of the country and repel the Israelis. I told my father I wanted to go and he did not believe me, telling me to stop joking as he had no time for silliness. I was dead serious and soon enough left with my friends to Lebanon on foot, sometimes clinging onto the back of buses, until we reached the Zabadani River in the south. It was just months before the Israeli invasion of Lebanon in 1982.

We arrived at a house occupied by some Palestinians from Shafa 'Amr. A girl drinking coffee on the balcony told us her name, Samira, and asked us what we were doing there. When we told her we had come from Yarmouk Camp in Damascus, she said she did not know where that was, but was kind enough to take us to see her father. Dawn was just breaking and he came out in his pyjamas. Taking one look at us, mere kids, he told us to go home and finish our studies. We refused to budge, instead insisting we were ready for the fight.

He took pity on us, maybe, and led us to a camp run by Salah Khalaf (Abu Iyad) for training. The camp was near Nabatiyeh, in a hilly area that was the perfect position to launch rocket attacks into Upper Galilee and perhaps hit some settlements. It was really breathtaking, so high up that at night you could see Palestine in the distance and the lights of Safad. We would spend hours each night trying to guess where the lights were shining from.

Our commanders were not that much older than we were, but they spoiled us rotten. Soon enough, we were trained in the use of arms and in digging tunnels deep in the ground to hide in. And so the days passed. On the day the Israelis invaded, we lost radio reception, and it was difficult to communicate. We knew the time had come. I was assigned to carry pots of rice and beans to the guerrillas manning the outpost, and I was about to do so when an explosion rocked the area near me. I dropped the pot and ran for cover and, as I ran, I heard someone shouting over a microphone: 'Evacuate the area. Surrender and you will be fine.'

We knew Israeli incursions were so meticulously planned that any tank advance would be preceded by paratroopers, combing the ground carefully so that even a snake would go underground for cover. But we did not feel so concerned, well not until the shelling intensified to such an extent that the ground shook under our feet. We hid in one of those caves we had dug for such an eventuality. There were 16 of us altogether, all hiding in the cave, from which we could see the main road leading to Nabatiyyeh A bomb exploded and a man's head was blown to pieces. It was the first time I had seen something like this.

Soon enough, the officer in charge of our group ordered us to attack the tanks. We had to obey. I crawled out behind the others. The Israeli soldiers were just metres away, but they did not see us. One was standing looking through a pair of binoculars. When we ventured out, I could not believe what I saw. There were tents blown apart, people dead and cars destroyed. I was beginning to feel alarmed and I did not want to go anywhere. But we had to continue creeping along our bellies towards the tanks. Then an explosion hit nearby and I thought I had died.

When I came to, I realized I had been wounded. I was carried into the cave along with three of my comrades, also wounded. For five days, we stayed there until we had exhausted all our water and food supplies, and had nothing left, but empty guns. A friend of mine bandaged my leg to stop the bleeding. Another guerrilla had some shrapnel in his hand. We could not take out the metal piece sticking out of his hand. It was too much for me. I began crying as I thought of my father and mother. I just wanted to go home. One of my friends tried to comfort me, telling me he would take me home.

On the fifth night, he said it was time to leave. I crept behind him and we reached a bombed-out building. There, we found some clothes and I changed into a pair of clean trousers. Then, we resumed creeping. It was dark and we did not realize we had crept right up to an Israeli tank.

Then things happened fast. An Israeli soldier pointed a gun at us and asked us to stand, but I could not stand. Then another came along and began to search us for weapons. We had nothing, of course. I looked at one of them, probably the leader, and felt relaxed looking into his face. I had been crying when I was in the cave, but when I saw this man I stopped crying, because I did not want to be called a coward. But deep inside, I just wanted to be with my mother. They took me to a hospital in Nabatiyyeh where I saw many of my comrades wounded and bandaged. I was taken to the operating theatre. When I came to, I realized I was in a civilian hospital and that the nurse tending to me was a Shi'ite Lebanese. There were no Israelis or anything and I thought I was dreaming, but then I saw the Israeli guard outside.

I told the nurse that I wanted my mother and asked whether she could go and get her to look after me. She did not reply. Within a few days, I was told that I was to be taken to Tel Aviv for further operations on my leg. Along with an old Lebanese fighter and two guerrillas, I was lifted by a helicopter, not inside, but held inside a cage hanging below the helicopter. I could only think they were going to drop us in the sea. It sounds like a movie when I talk about this, but I can see it so clearly. We were deposited on the roof of a building, and someone came along and shouted: 'You Arabs, you dogs.'

And then the interrogations and the psychological torture began. My interrogators would not believe I was 13, insisting I could not be older than nine. I was small for my age in those days. An officer called Murad came along. He spoke in an Egyptian dialect and he told me that my commander had surrendered, that everyone was in prison, including Yasser Arafat and George Habash. I told him I wanted to go back home to my parents. He kept on with questions. The interrogation sessions continued and we stayed for a while. There were some photographers who came to take pictures of us, 'the RPG kids', and it seemed that some Western journalists, seeing how young I was, canvassed for my release.

Within days, I was handed over to the Red Cross in Lebanon. Captain Murad, I must admit, was a fair man. When he handed me over, he gave me 500 dollars, looked me straight in the eye and told me: 'Kid, don't give up being a *fedayee*.' He even kissed me goodbye. This is the absolute truth, and I can never forget his kindness, particularly because what happened to me afterwards was much worse.

I was held by the Lebanese for about 50 days before they let me go. During my detention in Israel, I was slapped only once. You cannot believe how many lashings I got in Lebanon, and later on in Syria. I was a Fatah man, and I was imprisoned by the Syrians when Syria fell out with Arafat. I spent six years in a Syrian prison. Sometimes, I dream I am still in that prison. I have a constant fear of being followed and arrested. I look over my shoulder all the time. I sometimes think and question why God chose some people to be Palestinian, but I still thank him for choosing me to be one of them.

Notes

1. Mahmoud Darwish (1967) *Rita wa al-Bunduqiya* ['Rita and the gun'] in *Akher al-Layl* ['The End of the Night'], 2nd edn, Beirut: Dar al-'awda, pp. 45–7.
2. Rashid Khalidi (2006) *The Iron Cage*, Oxford: Oneworld Publications, p. 136.
3. Fatah dominated Palestinian politics until Arafat's death in November 2004. Arafat deserved much credit for getting the PLO recognized as the sole legitimate representative of the Palestinian people. However, this was undermined by the hollow structures of the PLO itself, which can in part be blamed on the deeply

ingrained habits of Yasser Arafat. For more details, see Khalidi, *The Iron Cage*, p. 144.

4. Ibid., p. 142.
5. The mystery surrounding Arafat's place of birth, life and aims continued to surround his persona up to his death in November 2004, when the ordinary facts of his life and birth were buried with him in his homeland. One story suggests he was born in Jerusalem; more reliable evidence indicates he was born in Gaza and grew up in Egypt. Another story says he was a member of the Jerusalem elite Husseini clan.
6. Abu Iyad with Eric Rouleau (1978) *My Home, My Land: A Narrative of the Palestinian Struggle*, New York: Times Books.
7. Yezid Sayigh (1997) *Armed Struggle and the Search for State*, Oxford: Oxford University Press, p. 71.
8. The Islamist movements took more of a hold in the Gaza Strip.
9. In 1964, Fatah took control of the Palestine Liberation Organization, which had been founded by the Arab League in 1960, confirming the group's political clout and national significance.
10. Israel also occupied the Golan Heights of Syria and the Sinai Peninsula up to the eastern bank of the Suez Canal.
11. Ilan Pappé (2006) *A History of Modern Palestine*, Cambridge: Cambridge University Press, p. 203.
12. Ibid., p. 187.
13. For more details, see Sayigh, *Armed Struggle and the Search for State*, p. 202.
14. The PLO's charter was changed during the fourth meeting of the Palestine National Congress in 1968, to adjust to the new political consensus and its revolutionary ideology: liberating Palestine through a people's war.
15. Tens of thousands of Palestinian and Arab volunteers joined the ranks of the Palestinian Revolutionary Movement within months of the battle, while the ideology of liberation caught the imagination of many across the Arab world. The battle started when about 15,000 Israeli troops, supported by helicopters and armoured vehicles, attacked the village of Karameh on the east bank of the Jordan River. Around 300 Fatah fighters stayed behind and were supported by Jordanian artillery. Although only 28 Israeli soldiers were killed, as opposed to 120–200 guerrillas, it was cast as a victory because the Israeli losses were relatively heavy.
16. Sayigh, Rosemary (1979/2007) *The Palestinians: From Peasants to Revolutionaries*, London: Zed Books, p. 158.

17. Rosemary Sayigh argues that, to understand the primary place of armed struggle among camp Palestinians, it is necessary to remember how many times the camps had been the targets for Israeli and Arab attacks. Ibid., p. 161.
18. Personal interview with Walid Salim al-Taybi in Beirut in August 2008.
19. The symbolic meaning of the *bunduqiya* ['gun'] changed dramatically when Arafat addressed the UN General Assembly in November 1974. He told the world: 'I have come bearing an olive branch and a freedom fighter's gun. Do not let the olive branch fall from my hand.'
20. For details of films of the revolution, see Nurith Gertz and George Khleifi (2008) *Palestinian Cinema: Landscape, Trauma and Memory*, Edinburgh: Edinburgh University Press.
21. Prison stories figure prominently in the self-representation of Palestinians inside the occupied territories and the Gaza Strip, because virtually everyone was affected by imprisonment.
22. John Collins (2004) *Occupied by Memory: The Intifada Generation and the Palestinian State of Emergency*, New York: New York University Press, p. 123.
23. Laila Khaled (2008). Personal interview with the author, Amman: August.
24. Haddad was a medical student at the American University of Beirut. He helped establish the Arab Nationalist Movement and had a direct role in planning the first PFLP hijacking.
25. Mohammed Naguib Mahmoud (2008). Personal interview with the author, Burj al-Barajneh Camp/Beirut: August.
26. Mohammad Naguib Mahmoud broke down crying in this interview.
27. Samira Salah (2008). Personal interview with the author, Beirut: August. Samira remains active in the Palestinian Women's Union and is a member of the Palestine National Council.
28. Samia Nasser Khoury (2007). Personal interview with the author, Beit Hanina/Jerusalem: November.
29. Beit Hanina is a Palestinian town just north of Jerusalem and part of the Jerusalem Governorate. In 1980, Israel annexed Jerusalem, thus dividing Beit Hanina into two parts, one considered to be in the West Bank and the other within the municipal borders of Jerusalem.
30. Ilan Pappé writes that Jerusalem was the first site of the first 'pilot project' of Jewish settlement on occupied territory. In early 1968, the Israeli authorities appropriated vast areas of East

Jerusalem, a third of which were private property, and re-zoned them as new Jewish suburbs. See Pappé (2006) *A History of Modern Palestine*, p. 194.

31. The Israeli campaign against political activity began in July 1967 with the expulsion from East Jerusalem of four notables who had called on the population to adopt Mahatma Gandhi's tactic of civil disobedience. Moshe Dayan, the Israeli Defence Minister, ordered the first act of collective punishment against the West Bank town of Qalqilya, demolishing half the houses in July 1967.

32. The university was closed 15 times in the years from 1974, for varying periods of time, the longest closure being four years, from 1987 to 1992, during the first Palestinian *intifada*. When the Israeli occupation authorities made Arab education illegal – which they often did, closing universities, schools and kindergartens – Palestinian education was pushed underground. Birzeit, like other universities, held classes covertly in homes, mosques and community centres. Carrying books was evidence of an 'illegal class' that could warrant arrest.

33. Samia was referring to the rift between Fatah and Hamas, which was at its worst following the electoral win by Hamas in the Palestinian elections in January 2006.

34. Hani Ahmad Issawi (2007). Personal interview with the author, 'Ezariyyeh/Jerusalem: November.

35. Karameh, a Jordanian village where Fatah had its headquarters, came under heavy attack by the Israeli Defence Forces on 21 March 1968, and this developed into a battle with Fatah. At the end of the battle, nearly 150 Fatah fighters, 20 Jordanian soldiers and 28 Israeli soldiers had been killed. Despite the higher Arab death toll, Fatah considered this a victory because of the rapid Israeli withdrawal. *Time* magazine, which covered the battle, put a picture of Arafat's face on the cover of its 13 December 1968 issue, catapulting him onto the world stage for the first time.

36. Israeli prisons are essentially political prisons for Palestinians suspected, accused and occasionally convicted of carrying out or planning acts of resistance, whether peaceful or armed. Within the pre-1967 borders, there are ten prisons, with nine more in the post-1967 occupied territories. There are regional detention centres and police stations used to detain suspects for interrogation and torture. Detention camps with only tents for shelter were also erected to house the large numbers of Palestinian prisoners held

during the 1982 invasion of Lebanon, the most notorious being Meggido, Ansar II (in Gaza) and Dhariyah.

37. Armon ha-Avadon prison is set behind a high wire fence on the last section of road from Jerusalem to Tel Aviv, about five miles [8 km] from Ben Gurion Airport. It was also one of the most notorious camps for detainees during the Palestinian uprising in 1936.

38. Zuhdi Hammoudeh al-'Adawi (2008). Personal interview with author, Yarmouk Camp/Damascus: August.

39. This is a reference to the first Palestinian–Israeli prisoner exchange in 1985, when 1,250 Palestinian prisoners were released and flown to Algeria.

40. His nickname refers to the new cultural hero that was beginning to challenge the dominant image of the *fedayee*. 'RPJ' means the anti-tank shoulder-mounted rockets that young Palestinians carried to slow down the Israeli advance in southern Lebanon in 1982. The image of the young martyr, the *shahid*, was suddenly brought into the limelight during the invasion, when over 650 Israelis died and 3,500 were wounded. Later on, in the West Bank and Gaza Strip, similar adolescents throwing rocks and taunting Israeli troops marked the rise of 'the children of the stones'. See Baruch Kimmerling and Joel Migdal (2003) *The Palestinian People: A History*, Cambridge, MA: Harvard University Press, p. 271.

41. Salah Mohammed (2008). Personal interview with the author, Yarmouk Camp/Damascus: April. This is one of the two people whose real names I changed for personal and security reasons.

CHAPTER FOUR

Living the Revolution: Living the Occupation, 1970–87

Extraordinary conditions foreground the ordinary, and the heroic consists in living every moment to the full. With shells exploding everywhere, the effort to maintain the primacy of the quotidian becomes a challenge to the bombs.... Sheer survival during a blitz assumes heroic proportions, and a walk on the streets... becomes an odyssey (Ibrahim Muhawi[1])

The Palestinian revolution began with high hopes of a return to Palestine, but within two decades it ended in tragedy: the death, injury and displacement of thousands, the destruction of homes and infrastructure, and eventually the evacuation of the *fedayeen* from Jordan and Lebanon.

The year 1970 brought with it the beginning of the end of the revolution, with the ousting of guerrilla factions from Jordan. There had been tension between Jordan and the various Palestinian groups over who controlled the streets and who represented the Palestinians, but relations deteriorated rapidly after militias from the Popular Front for the Liberation of Palestine hijacked three international flights and blew them up in the northern desert. When on 11 September 1970 a banner headline in Fatah's daily newspaper called for a 'revolutionary nationalist government', King Hussein of Jordan formed a military government, that declared martial law and ordered all Palestinian militia forces in cities and refugee camps to surrender their weapons. Armed conflict was inevitable.

At dawn on 15 September 1970, the Jordanian army struck with full force.[2] The 10-day civil war (known as Black September)[3] prompted a radical change in the PLO, which shifted its bases to Lebanon and began to develop a state-within-a-state there. Palestinian leaders set up headquarters in Beirut and military camps and bases were built in the south and south-west. Eventually, the PLO's control went far beyond the camps, and the guerrillas had nearly free rein in a wide swathe of Lebanese territory.[4]

In the context of long-standing rifts and worsening relations among Lebanon's various confessional groups, the Palestinians became involved into one of the bloodiest communal conflicts of the twentieth century, the Lebanese Civil War, lasting from 1975 to 1990 and resulting in more than 100,000 deaths and countless human tragedies.[5] Palestinian involvement in the war in Lebanon added another strand to Palestinian history and experience. The Christian Falangist militia attack in 1976 on the Tal al-Za'atar refugee camp in East Beirut, with the knowledge of the Syrians,[6] and the 1982 massacre of hundreds of Palestinians at the Sabra and Shatila camps, with the knowledge of the Israelis, underlined the vulnerability of Palestinians in exile.

While the liberal economic and political conditions of Lebanon allowed a small Palestinian middle class and bourgeoisie to do well, at least until the start of the civil war – indeed many Palestinians, especially Christians, were encouraged to purchase Lebanese citizenship – most of the Palestinians in Lebanon who left their homeland in 1948 lived in the camps and did not receive the same favourable treatment. And it was the 17 state-recognized camps – under Palestinian jurisdiction from 1969 to 1982 – that bore the brunt of the violence of the civil conflict and the subsequent Israeli attacks and invasions. In the end, it was Israel's devastating invasion in June 1982 – with its three-month siege of Beirut, the subsequent massacres in the Sabra and Shatila camps and the US-brokered PLO exit from the city – that signalled the end of the Palestinian revolution in Lebanon.

For more than two months, from 14 June to 23 August 1982, the Israelis and their Lebanese supporters surrounded and besieged the Palestinian factions and their nationalist Lebanese allies. Unlike previous Arab–Israeli wars, the invasion of Lebanon in the summer of 1982 cost the PLO its territorial base, its headquarters and the bulk of its military infrastructure. Eventually, Syrian-backed factions led a major split within Fatah and expelled from Lebanon the remaining forces loyal to the PLO and Fatah leader Yasser Arafat by the end of 1983.[7]

Although the USA and Lebanon pledged to guarantee the safety of those Palestinians left behind after the PLO was forced out on 23 August, Lebanese Christian militiamen, allied to Israel, massacred several hundred Palestinian civilians[8] at the Sabra and Shatila refugee camps between 16 and 18 September 1982. In 1985, Lebanese Shi'a militias from the Amal movement waged a savage war against the Palestinian camps in south and south-west Beirut, a conflict that peaked between 1985 and 1987 in what became known as the War of the Camps.[9]

Israel plays the field: Control in the occupied territories

Inside the occupied West Bank and Gaza Strip, after 1967, Palestinians had to cope with an aggressive Israeli occupation whose main objective was to gain control of the occupied lands and their resources without formally incorporating the Palestinian people into Israel as citizens of its parliamentary democracy.

The policies of the occupation included an expansion of Jewish settlements, with security and administrative links to Israel; restricting Palestinian control of the economy, even downgrading the economy itself; and suppressing resistance by the threat of extended jail terms, collective punishment, demolition of homes, censorship of the Palestinian press and deportation.[10] Together, these measures encouraged Palestinians to leave – many for high-paying jobs generated by the oil boom in the Gulf states – rather than submit to these policies.

The building of new settlements moved at breakneck speed. Between 1978 and 1987, the number of Jewish settlers grew by an average 5,960 a year. In terms of absolute numbers, there were 60,500 Jewish settlers in the West Bank in 1986, compared to 3,176 in 1976. On the eve of the 1987 *intifada*, 120 Jewish settlements of various sizes dotted the West Bank landscape. Other tactics aimed to stifle the Palestinian economy and labour market, and these hit the 844,000 refugees in the 27 camps in the occupied areas hardest, most acutely in the Gaza Strip, where the population density is nearly ten times that of the West Bank.

While the PLO was consolidating its presence in Lebanon, the leading Palestinians in the occupied West Bank and Gaza Strip put their energies into limited, local political initiatives and the creation of a variety of social organizations to aid grassroots efforts.[11] These strategies did not come to fruition easily, because the PLO at first refused to endorse them; but, with the reinstatement of local municipal structures, political struggle began to rival armed struggle as a tactical approach for dealing with the occupation.[12]

Palestinians differed in the way they showed their stead-fastness in the face of a prolonged occupation: some argued for preserving the status quo, with minimal interaction or co-operation with the enemy and opposition to demographic or territorial change, whereas others wanted active institution-building and saw local politics as a key component of the state-making process.[13] Although PLO leaders understood the importance of these measures and though Arafat personified Palestinian nationalism – he was nicknamed Mr Palestine – it was becoming increasingly clear that most Palestinians were not prepared to take up arms.

The 1982 Israeli invasion of Lebanon brought new dilemmas in the difficult relationship between Jews and Palestinians in Israel, particularly because the Palestinians identified with the PLO in a war that Israel claimed was meant to protect its northern territories, where Palestinians also lived; this caused resentment and anger among Jews. Eventually, it also brought about a shift to democratization, a process that matured after the 1982 war.[14]

Throughout the 1970s, the process of political participation and institution-building had already taken off, with Palestinians in Israel demanding equality in the Jewish state, an end to continuing land confiscation and withdrawal from the areas occupied in 1967. But, while supporting an end to Israel's occupation of the West Bank and Gaza Strip, their priority was to achieve equal status in the Jewish state[15] and control of the land, particularly when Israel granted officials favouring land expropriation a free hand after 1967.[16] Other concerns centred on Israel's main citizenship law (the Law of Return passed in 1950) which annulled the inherent right to citizenship normally granted to individuals born in a given territory.

In 1975, the Communist Party, which by then had expanded to incorporate non-communist Palestinian and non-Zionist Jewish bodies, formed the Democratic Front for Peace and Equality (*Jabha*), an umbrella organization built around the party that fielded a diverse list of parliamentary candidates, becoming the best representative of the interests of Palestinians inside Israel until the mid-1990s.[17] With this wider party base, thousands of Palestinians from all over the country took part in a landmark protest against land closure and expropriation in Sakhnin, a large Palestinian village in Lower Galilee, on 30 March 1976. Six Palestinian demonstrators were shot dead on what has since come to be remembered as 'Land Day',[18] a collective experience that had a profound effect on the whole community, uniting those inside Israel with Palestinians beyond the borders.[19]

1948 is not the past: The *Nakba* continues

There are too many events to remember and experiences to recount from the period 1970–87, which I call, as in the title of this chapter, 'Living the revolution, living the occupation'. Many regionally important developments did not seem to be relevant for the Palestinians I spoke to in various places: events such as the October 1973 Arab–Israeli War and even the 1979 Camp David peace treaty between Israel and Egypt, despite its

5   Life under occupation: At an Israeli checkpoint. Photograph: Ma'an News Agency.

momentous impact on the course of events and on geopolitical dynamics.

Most of those I interviewed wanted to tell of personal experiences and events that remain etched in their memories, not as past events, but as events that remain current because, to them, what happened in 1948 is not over. For them these events underline that the past is still present. To this day, Palestinian dispersion continues, the status of the refugees remains unresolved and living conditions, especially in the refugee camps in Lebanon, the occupied territories and Gaza Strip, remain dire. For those Palestinians, like myself, who have the good fortune to build decent lives elsewhere, whether in the United States, Kuwait, Lebanon or Britain, the pain of loss may be blunted; but, for those in Israel, the occupied territories and the Gaza Strip, or in the vicinity of Israel, the assault begun by Zionism against the Palestinians has not ceased,[20] suggesting that this is what may be so distinctive about the Palestinian experience of time and memory.[21]

Edward Said wrote that the one thing no Palestinian can forget is that 'violence has been an extraordinarily important aspect of our lives. Whether it has been the violence of our uprooting and the destruction of our society in 1948, the violence visited on us by our enemies, the violence we have visited on others or, most horribly, the violence we have wreaked on each other.'[22] This is violence that imposes itself as a constant state of emergency in people's daily lives, becoming the 'rule rather than the exception'.[23]

Some Palestinian intellectuals, artists and film-makers underline this continuous state of emergency by dwelling on images of suffering, resistance and steadfastness in their stories, films and poems. But it is perhaps Emile Habibi who has most profoundly portrayed the intensity and bleakness of life since 1948, ending his novella, *The Secret Life of Saeed: The Pessoptomist* (pessimist and optimist) with neither resolution nor redemption.[24]

Some of the personal accounts below, particularly those by refugees in Lebanon and Jordan, also dwell on personal suffering, their stories standing in stark contrast to those of the revolutionary period, which reflected high hopes and regeneration. The theme of personal suffering, some scholars argue, may have been influenced by the role of the primary organizations that took over the task of representing the Palestinians, particularly in Lebanon, after 1982: the many NGOs and UN bodies whose audiences are mostly foreign and whose motive is to portray Palestinians as victims who could benefit from the mobilization of world sympathy. This shift in representations of violent events is repeated in the narrated experiences of different forms of violence in Lebanon,[25] told mostly by women. Thinking about it, I wonder now whether talking about these painful events masks a desire to forget – for memory, as Freud tells us, is not only at the root of trauma but is also the source of its resolution.[26]

When the late Palestinian poet Mahmoud Darwish wrote about Israel's 1982 siege of Beirut, he attempted to purge the violence of (in Ibrahim Muhawi's words) 'the Lebanese phase of Palestinian history, the madness that was Beirut, as well as his attachment to the city, out of his system'.[27] His memoir is evocatively titled *Memory for Forgetfulness*, suggesting that in remembering he is also trying to block out a painful period of personal history. Former *fedayee* and now social worker 'Ahed, whose account I set out below, attempts to do the same, trying to bring closure to his experience of living the revolution. For memory scholar and French sociologist Maurice Halbwachs says it is the individual who remembers.[28]

In what follows, those individuals surviving traumas may not be able to remember or relate a coherent narrative because memories fall short of the requirements of history when society disappears and family members are absent.[29] Exact details of what happened, when, where and how are missing in the accounts of those refugees I interviewed in the various camps, particularly in Lebanon. Many I spoke to broke down in tears as they spoke of the present through the past. I found myself, despite my years of working as a journalist which included covering the 1982 invasion for Reuters News Agency, overwhelmed with emotions. I, too, shed tears and could not press my interviewees further.[30]

I start with Amal Nusseibeh's account of her memories of the September 1970 civil war in Amman. I then recount the stories of Fadila Khadir, 'Ahed and Makrama 'Awitah, all refugees in Lebanon, and of Miriam Shakir Sa'id in Wihdat Camp in Amman. I follow these stories of suffering with two stories by Palestinians under Israeli control; the first is the account of Na'ila Zayyad, the wife of the late Palestinian poet, writer, activist and politician Tawfik Zayyad, in Nazareth, and the second is the personal narrative of Bassam Shak'a, the former mayor of Nablus who lost both his legs in an attempted assassination in 1980. I end with two reflections, not stories, one by Mohammed Mughrabi about life under occupation in Jerusalem, and the last by Buthaina, who wanted to be identified by only her first name. She is a teacher in Yarmouk Camp in Damascus. Both are examples of the experience of trauma by proxy.

It is an unfinished story: Amal Nusseibeh[31]

My father was born in Jerusalem. He joined the Syrian Army in 1949 and was based in Aleppo, but I was born in Damascus in 1952. He left the army when the union between Syria and Egypt (in 1961) collapsed and moved to Jordan. I was 13 at the time. We grew up listening to Arab nationalist ideology and stories of the revolution. My brothers, who are much younger than me, were sent to training camps as teenagers.

1967 happened like a dream. At first, we thought the Arab armies had liberated Jerusalem, but then realized it was all a myth. Even the Golan Heights fell into Israeli hands. By that time, my father had joined Fatah as a volunteer as he had a job in a bank in the day. Within a few months, they asked him to join full time, and he devoted himself once again to military life. This was just before the 1970 civil war broke out and at a time when there were these claims that the Palestinians were forming a state-within-a state and things seemed to be getting out of hand in Jordan. I remember the day when armed militias blocked the street, preventing an official from visiting the-then Jordanian Prime Minister Abdel-Mun'em al-Rifa'i. My father did not condone this behaviour and insisted that the target was not Jordan, and yet he was jailed in 1970 because of his association with Fatah. Jordanian soldiers from al-Badiya stormed his offices and arrested him, just like that. It happened on a Friday. The clashes between the Palestinian factions and the Jordanian army started on the Thursday. My mother learned of his arrest through the radio.

We had given shelter to a group of *fedayeen* in our house, 25 of them, and they had used it as an office, not a base. We provided them with food, as many people in Amman at that time were doing. When the war started, they would rush out to tend to the injured and call for ambulances, but things got worse by the hour and they decided to leave and go into hiding. The fighting got out of control as battles raged on the street outside, and my mother was hit by a bullet while she was in the kitchen, the safest room in the house, where all our neighbours had taken to hiding in. A group of Jordanian soldiers were spraying our house with bullets. As we were running out for cover, I realized that she had not followed, so I went back to find her on the floor in a pool of blood, still gushing out of a wound near her heart. A water bottle had been hit, too, and was spurting out water. I turned back in fright to see my brother wounded, too, in the leg. He was not yet 18. I stripped my shawl and used it to cover her wounds. I shouted to the neighbours to tell the soldiers to stop shooting so we could evacuate the wounded. We could not leave all that day and night. I sat there that night beside my mother listening to the sound of air coming out of her back. The bleeding had stopped. One of our neighbours, an elderly woman, would not stop praying, reciting verses from the Koran.

They came back the next day to set fire to the house next door, claiming it was owned by a communist. One of our neighbours ventured out waving a piece of white cloth so they could stop the destruction. Still, they burst into the house, asking for the men folk. I told them my father was out of the country for work purposes. I could not say more. When they asked about my nationality, I said we were Syrian, which was kind of true because my father carried a Syrian passport. One of the soldiers said: 'You are worse than my shoes.' It felt like ages before anything happened, but it was really a few minutes before one of them who looked really humane relented and allowed me to take my mother to hospital. When the doctor saw her, he said: 'God loves your children for you to be able to survive this.' She had been hit by two bullets, one of them stayed inside her for eight years before it was removed. The fighting continued for a week. Our house was seriously hit. It was really difficult to cope at one point, with my mother and brother in hospital and my father in jail somewhere, and with me having to look after two younger siblings. I knew we had guns hidden somewhere in the house and I asked the neighbour to help me bury them, along with papers and books, in the garden. It feels like a film now, almost unreal and surreal. There we were busy digging in the dark, and there were the soldiers walking outside.

It was different in the past. My mother talked to us about Palestine and Jerusalem all the time, more than my father did, and we grew up with this deep identification with the land. My father adored Nasser, and I wish we had a leader like him now to move us out of this mess. It pains me to see what's happening now, the infighting, the indecision, the situation in Gaza. I am fine and comfortable here in Amman. For many people, the story seems to have finished, but it has not. It continues.

Tal al-Za'tar: Fadila Khadir[32]

My life is about living in camps, a permanent refugee. I hope it will be better for my children. I was brought up in Tal al-Za'tar Camp ['the Hill of Thyme'],[33] which we left in 1976 to Burj al-Barajneh in West Beirut. In the late 1960s and early 1970s, we lived a normal life though we had some difficulties moving in and out of the camp. There were always problems and the Lebanese civil war had started.

During the 1970 clashes in Jordan, the Palestinian resistance began underground activities here, mobilizing people on a large scale. Some, like me, did not train in the use of arms, but we had lessons in ideology and first aid. I cannot remember how things started to get worse, but the Syrians helped in the attacks by the Lebanese Falangist Christian militias on the camp. At the beginning, there were clashes at checkpoints, kidnappings and killings.[34]

This state of affairs, of sporadic battles, kidnappings and sniping, continued for two years until the siege of the camp in 1976. During the siege of the camp, I worked alongside a group of women to help the wounded, but we ran out of medical supplies and had to use table salt to clean the wounds. When the fighting got worse, there were no more places to bury the dead. I remember making bread in one room and swollen corpses lying in the next. The siege of the camp lasted for seven months. When the camp fell on 12 August 1976, thousands had died. The shelling was relentless throughout. Still, we tried to continue with our normal lives, organizing classes for our children in the evening because it was safer then to group them and teach them.

When the camp fell, I saw people running out of their houses, militiamen running to shelters in the hills or anywhere they could go to. Some young men were stripped naked as they did not want to be identified. We did not know what to do as we no longer were a community, but broken souls. We walked out along with the others hoping to get to the Red Cross which would guarantee our safety. Our group was mostly composed of women and girls. As the eldest in my family, I led my siblings out. The Red Cross was nowhere to be found, and all the while, the line of people leaving grew longer and bigger.

People were in shock, telling us horrible stories about how they survived. One woman said she was asked to choose which one of her four children to be killed. She had obviously lost her mind as she

kept repeating the story again and again. There were stories of torture, like that of Abu 'Ayyad's. Even now, as you can see, mentioning
his name and thinking of what happened to him makes me cry. When
I returned to the camp after seven days, I could not find my father.
He had disappeared, maybe kidnapped or killed, like many others.
I went to Beirut to look for other members of my family. They were
also looking for me, and had given up looking, thinking I had died.
But by a miracle of God's, we managed to find each other and pick
up the pieces. These are difficult stories to tell and there are many
more, because that was not the end to our suffering. Can you imagine
there were these places where they would keep chopped heads and
where people could go and identify whether these were of relatives
or friends? I could not bear to go look for my father there.

Our problems have not ended. The PLO left and left us alone,
with no money, no compensation, nothing. I am in a better position
than many others. I know one of the women in the camp here who
had to give birth to each of her children in different countries. At
least, I have stayed put. In 1985, my older brother was killed in the
Camp Wars, and another went missing in 1982. He was 16 years
old and we later found out he had been taken prisoner by Israel.
You have to live with this because otherwise, if you keep thinking
and remembering, you might go mad with grief. My sister did lose
her mind when she heard that my brother Fu'ad had died. It is not
unusual to have a martyr in each family. Some families have four.
That is not a problem, but *the problem is that we are no longer a
community* (her emphasis). Perhaps it is our fault because we left
our homeland in the first place.

Can all this be for Palestine?
'Ahed's Story[35]

Every revolution needs sacrifices. Our revolution needed sacrifice,
and there were many martyrs. It ended when we were no longer
ready to sacrifice, when we were weary of the revolution forever
taking and not giving us anything back. And it ended when our
leadership walked away from us.

I was ten years old when I joined the armed struggle. I was so enthusiastic that I used to escape from school to train in the use of arms and take part in activities to do with the struggle. We had so much hope. Now, you look at your country on television screens and you realize that those who took it by force are there to stay.

I am one of those people, like many others, who was deeply influenced by my parents and grandparents and their memories of the homeland. When you hear them talk about life there, you are bound to be committed and not to give up. They speak of its beauty, of its goodness and of their happy times: it sometimes feels a delusion. Those who paid for this idea, this delusion, are the refugees in the camps here in Lebanon. Other refugees in Syria or Jordan would tell you they want to return and have all of Palestine back. That's because they have a comfortable life. Here, it is different. Ask a Palestinian here and he would tell you that we just need a space to breathe in. And all of this humiliation is for this idea called Palestine. I shall tell you a story before I tell you about the past. I applied for an identity card for my new-born son Hammouda, and they insisted on putting the word 'refugee' next to his name. A newly born and he already has a label, a refugee!

I fought alongside other Palestinian guerrillas and the Lebanese leftist groups during the civil war, in the 1970s and 1980s. I was in Beirut in 1982 during the Israeli invasion, too. In those days, we did not seem to care whether we died or not. Now, I thank God I did not become a martyr because it would have been a waste. I would have gone into oblivion. I am glad I did not lose any limb or organ because I would have been begging by now. I was wounded by shrapnel in my leg, my arm and my head, but that was all. My father was martyred in 1986 when he was hit by shrapnel while he was trying to get some flour. We were under siege during the camp wars. Those were hard days because those who got injured had to manage and find a way of surviving or they had to die, alone. Ordinary people suffered, but our leadership got away.

Everybody will tell you it is difficult being a Palestinian refugee in Lebanon. You almost feel you are a criminal, a half human. With no armed struggle to hold onto and belong to, you are nothing. This is the reality. You go to Shatila Camp now and you see young men sitting smoking the 'hubble-bubble' because there is nothing to do. Today, I laugh at people who continue to talk about the revolution and say they want to carry guns. I tell people it is time to forget.

I did not come here of my own free will: Makrma 'Awitah[36]

I was born in the village of al-Kabri[37] in Galilee in 1941. A third of our village inhabitants ended here in Lebanon because of its proximity to the Galilee. It was like next door, and I never forget how generous the Lebanese were to open their doors for us. We left our homes because we heard that the Jewish militias were massacring people in Haifa and that many people had been killed. So we fled along with the rest first to Tarshiha, then to Nazareth and then here. I regret this to this very day because all this suffering and misery we have lived through was a result of our departure from the homeland.

We were peasants and lived off the land and livestock. The streets were narrow, so if a tank rumbled through, it would block the road. A battle did take place in our village and some Jews were killed. Their names are engraved in rock, which I saw with my own eyes when I went to visit after 50 years. I took my daughter and granddaughter with me and showed them everything and told them all the stories. They could hardly believe what they saw. The Jews had built a settlement right behind our house and used it as a base for attacks. No other people have experienced what we Palestinians have. And this is because we left Palestine. Had we stayed behind, nothing would have happened to us. But I did not come here out of my own free will. I was forced out by Israel.

My memories are of a continuous tragedy. First there was *al-Nakba*; then the Lebanese civil war, then the Israeli invasion and then the fighting with Amal (the Lebanese Shi'ite group). When we finished with that battle, we began to fight amongst ourselves. That was the worst. One of my sons was wounded during the

Camp Wars, the other went to Sweden and another, Mohammed, is in Denmark. He lost his mind because of what he witnessed. I helped him get away, giving him the savings earned through making clothes for people. I saw my nephew die, he was 17. When I visit his grave, I feel nothing. During those difficult days of war, I did not leave – because leaving, as we did in 1948, would mean total loss.

I remember how Yasser Arafat, God rest his soul, a maverick man who swings around himself 70 times ([euphemism meaning he is clever, but devious], fired up our young men and women with passion, then left us in the lurch. I don't believe in any talk of armed struggle anymore. A hand grenade here, a bomb there, or shooting someone leads to nowhere. We only need education. My children feel the way I do and regret carrying arms for nothing. In fact, if we carried our weapons for the cause, for Palestine, we would have won, but we carried it to become heroes in other people's lands.

I never feared anyone but God. I was wounded twice during the camp wars. A bullet entered my hand on one side and came out the other. I cannot remember the year as my memory is fading. It might have been 1986. My husband was still alive then, but many people, women and the elderly died because of the lack of food. I was not afraid. Each party was trying to impose its own rules, while Syria was waiting on the sidelines waiting to jump in. I know that a Jew would always help another Jew. We Palestinians do not do that and I cannot understand why. My head spins when I think about this. We do not help each other. I hope my grandchildren have a better life.

It is a scent you never forget: Miriam Shakir Said[38]

I got married in 1970, one week before the civil war began. My husband was a soldier in the Jordanian army, which posed problems for us as a family. I cannot talk much about this because walls have ears.

That war was terrible and hard. There were corpses on the street, some of them left rotting for more than a week. We had no medicine to give the wounded; no water to drink. Ten days after the war began, some of the guerrilla fighters brought us cans of water to drink. When the fighting ended, they took all the corpses to the UNRWA headquarters, then they buried them in the ground along with their useless weapons. A pregnant woman in her eighth month lay bleeding in the street and we could not help in fear of getting shot. She and her child died. I remember this sight to this very day.

The fighting lasted for 12 days. We came out of our shelters, but the battle was not over. The soldiers continued to come and search for wanted people. They took all males above 12 years old to prison. My brother was one of them and he was kept in detention for 40 days. He was an only brother. I cannot tell you who was at fault, but we heard that there were thousands who wanted to be in charge in Jordan. Some people tell me now that the Palestinians wanted to take over. We were living in Hussein Camp, the hardest hit. But they tell me that in Wihdat Camp every household was affected.

We are originally from Lydd and my parents left in 1948 first to a place called Dura al-Qara' near Jericho. At that time, my mother had three boys and one girl. Two of the boys died with typhoid fever because the water was contaminated. They came to Hussein Camp and stayed in the tents until 1956 when UNRWA gave each refugee family a room, with no bathroom, mind you. There was a public toilet that was used by all the families living along two streets. I remember those days. We had to fill up tanks for our water supplies. Men could not find work, so we lived on aid.

In 1964, they built schools in the Nuzha area in Amman and we started going to school. These were originally tents, and then they were built out of stone. We were keen to study although we felt that we also learnt much from the elderly. They knew everything and I remember the stories my mother told us about Lydd and its factory. When I went to visit in 1974, I saw it there and it was an olive grinding factory. It was a visit to remember and savour. As you stand on the ground, you smell this very peculiar scent, a mixture of thyme and something else, a fragrance, a perfume. And it is a scent you can never forget.

Nazareth was the 'imagined Palestine' in Israel: Na'ila Zayyad[39]

I was born in 1946 two years before Nazareth and its surrounding villages were occupied, in mid-July 1948. I am originally from the Sabbagh family, but I married Tawfiq Zayyad, the well-known Palestinian poet and leader when I was 20. And in those days that was something for a Christian woman to marry a Muslim man. We have four children.

My earliest memories are of growing up in a house of communists, but it was Tawfik and his commitment to Palestine that was the centre of my life. Those were beautiful days of resistance and hope. I tell the young today that they need to live under military rule to know what sacrifice means, what hardship is and what it means to hear the army knocking at your door at four in the morning.

I was a baby in 1948 and my first real memory of a momentous event, and there are many, was the Suez Crisis in 1956. Though it was kilometres away, it felt the attack was happening next door as we listened to news and developments on the radio. Another of my earliest memories was when my father was arrested. It was the tenth anniversary of the creation of Israel, in May 1958, when the military rulers decided to hold celebrations here in Nazareth behind the Roman Church. The Communist Party, which my father belonged to, called a protest and the police came to our house with an order to arrest him.

I was young, but I went along with others to protest outside the prison gates calling for his release, and the release of friends and family members. With many of our young men folk in prison, women and young people would take part in protests even though all protests were banned under military rule. We were the first people to throw stones at the occupation forces in 1958. I was 12 and it was during those turbulent and exciting times that I understood what it meant to be occupied and how important it was to resist.

I was influenced by my father, an ardent anti-Zionist. I did not have a normal childhood because it felt I spent much of those early days going to lectures, attending cultural events by the Communist Party, which by 1967 had become the most significant political party within the Palestinian minority in Israel. I also read key works by writers and poets like Emile Habibi, Mahmoud Darwish and Samih al-Qassem, and, later, my husband's. We also read world resistance literature though some books were banned as the military rulers felt the written word was a weapon and insisted that all poems, stories and words had to be vetted by the military censor.[40]

I joined the Communist Youth Party at an early age. My job was to distribute leaflets and mobilize the crowds. We called a protest in 1964 on the anniversary of the 1956 massacre of Kafr Qassem, in which 49 villagers were killed. As we walked to the city centre, a large police force blocked our way. I was walking with Juhaina, Emile Habibi's daughter, and we had been instructed not to look back but to continue walking. So we walked straight into the Israeli police cordon, only to be beaten up and arrested. Even handcuffed, I continued to shout anti-Israeli slogans and singing some nationalist songs. I will never forget this Israeli policeman who continued to beat us even as we arrived at the police station. It was sometimes humiliating because we were threatened and told that if we did not co-operate we would have no work, food or permits to move around.

I got married in 1966, and my daughter was two weeks old when the 1967 war broke out. Within half an hour of declaring the start of the war, the Israelis knocked at the door and took Tawfik away to jail. Eventually, I got used to them coming and taking him to prison or questioning him. That time, they did not keep him for long, just for 21 days. After the 1967 war, Palestinians from the West Bank would come and visit with the green line no longer divisive. They would say 'you eat honey in Israel,' but this was not the case.

The 1967 defeat was a big blow, but we continued to hold meetings and mobilize despite the threat of house arrest. Our strategies had changed by then as we wanted to have a voice in Israel and break the silence. We tried to meet other Palestinian leaders in the West Bank, but Tawfik was not allowed to leave Nazareth, nor visit the West Bank until he became a member of the Israeli Knesset.

We knew that the best formula for co-existence was the idea of two states for two people based on Israel's withdrawal to the pre-1967 boundaries and continued to insist on this until it was adopted by the Palestine Liberation Organization. Having lived under Israeli rule for 18 years, we knew there was no magical formula, no throwing the Jews in the sea or wiping Israel off the map.

Tawfik was elected mayor of Nazareth in 1975 despite pressure from the Israelis to field their own candidates and give them the post. He received 69 per cent of the votes. I remember one American newspaper reporting the news under the headline 'Red Star over Nazareth.' It was then that our real struggle began, through political means and the media. We took over the municipality and began serious work, and it was like nothing before. People were sceptical of the changes and said nothing would happen, but we persevered. Things had been bad in Nazareth and we needed people to engage with us and work towards improving living conditions and services without buckling in to Israel or losing our Palestinian identity. We established a volunteer camp and encouraged the youth, men and women, to join. Those were beautiful days because everybody worked together as a community. It felt like we were a micro-state in Nazareth.

When I talk about my memories, I cannot but talk of Tawfik because he embodied what it means to be Palestinian in Israel. He continued to struggle against occupation, to raise the standards of living here, achieve equality in education and secure jobs for the Palestinians. During the *intifada* of 1987, we mobilized people to collect contributions to the West Bank and Gaza during their moments of strife. We helped the internally displaced refugees, some of whom ended in Nazareth, adjust to displacement and made them feel welcome. Nazareth *was* the 'imagined Palestine' within Israel.

The Israelis exerted pressure on us, as they always do, as they were beginning to be worried about the popularity of the Communist Party and its support base, but people like good leadership, and Tawfik was a good and charismatic leader. His speeches were compared with Gamal 'Abdel-Nasser's. He was elected to the Knesset in the 1973 elections on the list of Rakah, the Israeli Communist Party, and began pursuing the government to change its policies towards the Palestinian Arabs. He defended women's equal rights in society, standing up to Islamist elements asking that women should not walk with men. At home, he was the perfect gentleman. When he would come home, he would ask about the children, wonder whether they had studied enough, then ask about me. He made me feel equal to him in every way. I am sorry, but this was my experience that has made me what I am. I still feel the trauma of his death, 13 years ago. He was killed on 5 July 1994 in a head-on collision in the Jordan Valley on his way back to Nazareth from Jericho, where he went to meet Yasser Arafat.

All my memories are of politics: Bassam al-Shak'a[41]

Bassam al-Shak'a was the elected mayor of Nablus between 1976 and 1982. Nablus has a long history of political activism when it played a critical role in the earlier uprisings of the 1930s. In the early twentieth century, Nablus played the parochial foil to Jaffa's cosmopolitanism.[42] Months before it was occupied by Israel in 1967, the city witnessed a revolt against the Hashemite regime when mass demonstrations were organized and about 20 inhabitants killed by the Jordanian security forces. Nablus seemed to be the ideal base for guerrilla activities, with its winding alleys and densely populated Kasbah (core), and its hinterland of remote, mountain villages.

It seems all my memories are of politics and activism. I opened my eyes to the revolution of 1936, though I do not remember the events well as I was six years old at the time. The *mujahideen* would come to our house as it was near the cemetery where they would hide and I used to give them water to drink.

I am the tenth child in a family of eleven. I was in the ninth grade at *al-Najah al-Wataniyah* School when the catastrophe happened, but even at that age I decided to join *Jaysh al-Inqadh* (The Arab Liberation Army) with some friends my age. We abandoned our books and went north in secret, making our way on foot towards Lebanon and then Syria where we stayed for a while. We fought a battle with the Jews, but were not able to do much when the English intervened. 1948 left us frustrated and devastated and, realizing that we lacked any form of serious military organization, I became active on the political front. All my memories are about political activism.

Pan-Arab nationalism was popular in the 1950s, particularly after the Free Officer revolution in 1952 that toppled the monarchy in Egypt. When Egypt and Syria united, we were so enthusiastic and hopeful that something might happen and we would defeat Israel and get back the land. When the union collapsed and following the Jordanian government's attempts to break up the nationalist movement, many of our leadership went underground. I was one of them. I hid here in the Nablus area before going to Beirut and then to Syria. Then I went to Egypt for six years with my wife, a colleague and comrade in the Arab Ba'ath Party, which I had joined by then. We came back in 1965, but I was jailed by Jordan in 1966 following the events of al-Sammou'[43] along with three of my brothers. I was freed after 25 days.

I cannot talk about myself as a person because I am part of a collective. My individuality is nothing without this collective, so my memories of events, such as the 1967 war, are seen through this 'collective' lens. After the defeat, I immediately started a campaign to stop people from leaving their homes, as they did in 1948. By that time, the Israeli plan to force people out was becoming clear – they actually did force people out of Qalqilya. We co-operated with the then mayor of Nablus, Hamdi Kan'an, to encourage people to stay. In the early days of the occupation, our aim was to resist Israeli policies, including their plans to build settlements near Nablus, impose councils as our legal representative, instead of the PLO, and destroy our unity.

I was elected mayor of Nablus in 1976, through a popular vote. I was to remain mayor until 1982. Our people elected the national list in all the cities in the occupied territories, which the Israelis fought from the beginning as they wanted the councils to accept the occupation and military rule. They controlled everyday life, and deported two mayors in the territories at the beginning of 1980. After that they tried to kill three mayors by using car bombs. I was one of them.

I had a premonition they might harm me and was debating whether to go spend some time with a friend in Ramallah, but I decided to leave my life in the hands of God. That morning, I was waiting for my daughter Ghadir to come out of the house. I started the engine when the car exploded. It was so strange, the whole thing. I remember seeing my hands covered with blood and having no feelings in my legs. I screamed to a man standing by to tell Um Nidal (my wife) to call for an ambulance, but I knew they might have cut off the phone lines. It was so imperative to go to hospital straight away.

When I came to, I had already lost both of my legs. The mayor of Ramallah lost his foot and the muscles in his other leg, while the mayor of El Bireh was lucky as he had heard about the incidents in Nablus and Ramallah, and did not use his car. They wanted to take me to Israel for treatment, but I refused. Finally, we got a permit to go to Jordan, thanks to my wife who left no stone unturned. I arrived in Amman with the blood not yet dry and stayed there for a month before going to London for further treatment. The Israelis never even made an investigation and nobody asked me for information about the bombings. Some settlers were arrested, but they were really guests of the Israeli authorities in those prisons.

Israel dismissed most of the elected councils in 1982 and began to administer the area by force, removing elected mayors of municipalities. They refused to hold elections and tried to oblige us by force to accept the civilian administration until the *intifada* of 1987. It was the answer to the occupation. The Israeli occupiers believe this land is theirs, use our land, our water, even limit the use of water and electricity so that we are forced to leave. When I was mayor, we fought for a license to develop our own electricity station, and we implemented a programme to clean the water to use for agriculture, but they made problems and stopped us. We had problems building schools, but we managed to. Of course, all universities and schools were shut during the uprising, but we began other methods to keep going, teaching at homes and in secret. We remain under occupation. In the paper today, they say Palestinian Authority forces enter Nablus to impose order and law, but security remains controlled by Israel.

Life goes on: Mohammed Mughrabi[44]

I was born in *Harat al-Magharbeh* in Jerusalem in 1966. Within a year of my birth, the neighbourhood lost its identity and the area flattened. My mother would always repeat the story of how terrified she was when she heard the Israelis had won the war and how, in her fright, she carried the pillowcase instead of me. Some people left their homes, but they could not return.

We moved to Salah al-Din Street in Jerusalem and stayed there for a while. Soon, we realized that the occupation was to stay, and we became used to protests, Israelis, soldiers, jeeps and the press everywhere. I was always interested in art, inspired by a teacher called Miss Sonia at the Dar al-Awlad school, a traditional school. In those days, we were not allowed to use colours of the Palestinian flag. We had to play by the rules. Even in drawing, they (the Israelis) interfered. I used to go to Arab clubs and attend some events there, but we were always short of funds. Sometimes, we did not have pencils to draw or write with. We thought at the time that perhaps Palestinian artists and writers living beyond the green line, that is pre-1948 Palestine, were immune to all these restrictions, but soon we found out they actually had undergone the same treatment and discrimination. I began to visit and with time meet with some Israeli artists because I did not feel the need to remain isolated. But they seemed to have a prescribed picture in their mind of what an Arab should be like. With time, they accepted me, and it was then that I was allowed to use all colours.

Those were the days before the *intifada*, but at the beginning of 1986, there was a feeling that Israelis, any one of them, was scared of us Arabs. They began to tighten the siege and soldiers would examine all our bags, stopping us arbitrarily. I could no longer go to the Israeli Museum to draw or exhibit because I could not carry my paint with me. Things were beginning to get worse and people did not go to work except for an hour in the morning. I really don't want to give the wrong impression, because while we were living all these problems and tragedies, while the occupation tightened the noose, we found ways to be happy, to laugh and have fun. In the course of one day, you could start your day with some sadness because of an event or something and then attend a wedding in the evening. I felt, and perhaps because of my artistic nature, that we Palestinians did not really want to live the misery and that happiness was also part of us.

We had our dreams, our lives and got on with our lives, but, of course, the tragedy of the occupation was there in the background, a daily reminder of who we were and what could happen to us. How can you not be affected when you see another house demolished here and another family left homeless just like that, for no reason? How can you not despair when you see Palestinians, like yourself, fleeing the country in their thousands because of this occupation? Some people do not return and will never return because all they want from their home is security and safety.

I have stayed put, trying to live a reasonable life so that my daughter Miriam, only four, can have a life and a future and so that she could one day move freely, as is her right. I want to see a time when she does not need all these cards to show and to prove her existence. It is sad, though, because all I can see of Palestine is a dream.

I know Palestine is only a dream: Buthaina[45]

I have always been dreaming. In fact, there are two main dreams I used to have and I remember one of them vividly. This is the one in which Palestine is Paradise, a place unlike any other in the world, and because it is unlike any other, it denies you the ability to call anywhere home.

6 Six-year-old Noor lives in Jal al-Baher in Tyre, Lebanon, a collection of 450 makeshift dwellings on the edge of the sea. The dwellings were built in 1951 by Bedouin Palestinians intending to maintain their lifestyle as they resisted settlement in the camps. Children, like Noor, spend hours playing during the summer. Photograph: Tanya Habjouqa.

This idea has been planted in my mind by my parents, particularly my father who would often tell us: '*Ya awlad* (you kids), think how beautiful Syria is, how beautiful Tartus is, and imagine that Palestine is even more beautiful.' How could it not be Paradise? In my dream of Palestine as Paradise, I would imagine myself swimming to reach Palestine and that Palestine had no borders. And I felt that if we returned, we would return swimming. The fact that we cannot return to it, even swimming, is too painful to think about.

The second dream is the one connected with the 1982 Israeli invasion of Lebanon, and it is one that I don't like to remember. I used to dream that one day I would join the Palestinians fighting off the Israelis. The invasion of 1982 ended that dream. The invasion of Lebanon, the attacks on Sabra and Shatila, the departure of the PLO was a nightmare. When I saw the Palestinian forced exodus from Beirut I could not understand why it happened and how. I was very young, about six years old, but even at that age I wondered why they had to leave, why they did not remain, and then wondered why my grandparents' and parents' generation did not remain in Palestine.

I grew up, like many of my contemporaries here in Yarmouk Camp, in a family of nationalists. My father not only talked about Palestine, but carried it in his blood. He was a soldier with the Syrian army and took part in the 1973 October war, and got wounded, but only after he managed to help destroy four Israeli tanks. He wanted to continue fighting despite his injury to his shoulder. It was not only his zeal. In our household, Palestine was with us for breakfast, lunch and dinner. My grandmother would never stop talking about Saffuriyyeh, where she comes from, about its beauty, about the pomegranate trees and the church. Though Muslim, she went to a convent to study. And I would imagine myself there, in the open spaces and the fields, and try and move out of this existence in the camp, with its narrow alleys, small rooms and basic schools.

I was born in 1976, so I lived the Palestinian experience in Lebanon in my childhood. I lived this experience as though I was there. I cried with those people I saw crying on television, shouted with others screaming at the Arabs to help; and cursed the attackers and wished them a horrible fate. Of course, it is not the same as others who actually lived them, but I experienced living them, too, from a distance. I experienced this because these events reminded me of why my parents left Palestine in the first place and why I was destined to be a Palestinian.

Like other Palestinian families, particularly in the camps, we suffered and lost some of our relatives. Some of my cousins are martyrs. Some died before I was born. We are constantly reminded of their sacrifice and we have their photos in their youth carrying their guns on the wall in our house. I followed the news on the radio and later on television, and Palestine, my imagined Palestine, became bigger and bigger, as it also became Lebanon, and then Syria when the Fatah split took place and the Syrians turned against those Fatah supporters, and then it was Palestine again during the first and second *intifadas*.

How can you forget? I am not talking about the right of return. This is not what it means to be Palestinian is about. Return is a dream, too. I am talking about the living conditions of the Palestinians; the daily suffering and the humiliation people encounter on a daily basis. We in Syria have comfortable lives and live well, even as refugees, but our problem is that we are living in Syria and not in our country. It is not return, but it is like this something inside me (us) that has not happened yet. It is like I am waiting for something or for me to turn into someone else. I know it is a dream, but I try to turn it into reality by teaching my students about it. And as I talk and talk, I realize that it is no longer a dream, but a belief. It is a belief that stems not from the belief that there is a land and a country, but the belief that this land is occupied and has been taken by force.

Notes

1. Ibrahim Muhawi (1995) 'Introduction' in Mahmoud Darwish (trans.), *Memory for Forgetfulness*, Berkeley: California University Press, p. xv.
2. For more details of the developments that led to the civil war in Jordan and the war itself, see Yezid Sayigh (1997) *Armed Struggle and the Search for State*, Oxford: Oxford University Press.
3. The civil war in Jordan was called Black September by the Palestinians. Refugee camps bore the brunt of the ten-day battle, in which between 3,000 and 4,000 people were killed, 10,000 wounded and 50,000 made homeless, according to an estimate by a Norwegian spokesman for Save the Children Fund, quoted by Reuters on 22 October 1970.
4. The Lebanese police all but disappeared from the streets and the old leadership in the camps began to feel vulnerable.
5. Baruch Kimmerling and Joel S. Migdal (2003) *The Palestinian People: A History*, Cambridge, MA: Harvard University Press, p. 268.
6. Syria, which had been Fatah's main ally, proved to be its key enemy when it supported Fatah dissidents to enhance its own regional ambitions and deal with its own concerns. See Helena Lindholm Schulz (1999) *The Reconstruction of Palestinian Nationalism: Between Revolution and Statehood*, Manchester: Manchester University Press, p. 45.
7. Sayigh, *Armed Struggle and the Search for State*, p. 545.

8. Some figures suggest 800 people were killed, but the number remains disputed.

9. The camp wars turned the Palestinians into *mustabaheen* ['a group left unprotected'], vulnerable to the attacks by the Lebanese Amal movement.

10. Samih Farsoun and Christina Zacharia (1997) *Palestine and the Palestinians*, Boulder, CO: Westview Press, p. 227.

11. See Kimmerling and Migdal (1994/2003) *The Palestinian People: A History*.

12. Sara Roy (1989) 'The Gaza Strip: critical effects of the occupation' in Naseer Aruri (ed.) *Occupation: Israel over Palestine*, Belmont, MA: Association of Arab-American University Graduates, p. 259.

13. For further details, read Kimmerling and Migdal (1994/2003) *The Palestinian People: A History*.

14. Ilan Pappé (2006) *A History of Modern Palestine*, Cambridge: Cambridge University Press, p. 226.

15. Ibid., p. 224.

16. Jews were encouraged and asked to settle in the Galilee in every possible way: in new towns, new *kibbutzim* and new community centres.

17. The DFPE provided the Palestinian community in Israel with the ability to express political views and an identity that was not compelled to pay lip service or subordinate itself to the Zionist agenda.

18. The events, coupled with the success of the *Rakah* (communist) party in defeating Zionist lists in the 1975 municipal elections in Nazareth, ushered in a higher stage of awareness and unity among Palestinians in Israel.

19. Nadim Rouhana (1997) *Identities in Conflict: Palestinian Citizens in an Ethnic Jewish State*, New Haven, CT: Yale University Press, p. 68.

20. Ahmad Sa'di and Lila Abu-Lughod (2007) *Nakba: Palestine, 1948, and the Claims of Memory*, New York: Columbia University Press, p. 19.

21. Lena Jayyusi (2007) 'Iterability, cumulativity, and presence' in Sa'di and Abu-Lughod (2007) *Nakba: Palestine, 1948, and the Claims of Memory*.

22. Edward Said (1986) *After the Last Sky*, London: Vintage, p. 5.

23. Walter Benjamin said: 'the state of emergency in which we live is not the exception but the rule.' For the full quotation, see John Collins (2004) *Occupied by Memory: The Intifada Generation and the Palestinian State of Emergency*, New York: New York University Press, pp. 5–6.

24. This is the story of a Palestinian who has been permitted to return to his home town, Haifa, after the *Nakba* and who becomes an Israeli citizen. His return is made possible after he agrees to work as a collaborator with the Israelis. Significantly, the first letter the narrator receives from the ill-fated Saeed pleads, 'Please tell my story.'

25. Laleh Khalili (2007) *Heroes and Martyrs of Palestine: The Politics of National Commemoration*, Cambridge: Cambridge University Press, p. 161.

26. Sigmund Freud, in one of his later works (1920/1991), explains that the pain of reliving events that lead to trauma may in turn hold the key for a gradual return to normality. Cited and paraphrased in Haim Bersheeth (2007) 'The continuity of trauma and struggle: recent cinematic representations of the Nakba' in Sa'di and Abu-Lughod (eds) *Nakba: Palestine, 1948*, p. 162.

27. Muhawi (1995) 'Introduction' in Darwish (trans.) *Memory for Forgetfulness*, p. xxi.

28. Maurice Halbwachs (1980) *Collective Memory*, New York: Harper & Row.

29. Diana Allan (2007) 'The politics of witness: remembering and forgetting 1948' in Shatila Camp in Sa'di and Abu-Lughod (eds) *Nakba: Palestine, 1948*, p. 249.

30. Rosemary Sayigh (1979/2007) *The Palestinians: From Peasants to Revolutionaries*, London: Zed Books.

31. I spoke to Amal at her home in Amman in August 2008.

32. Fadila Khadir (2008). Personal interview with the author, Burj al-Barajneh Camp/Beirut: August.

33. The camp housed about 60,000 Palestinian refugees and was administered by the UN.

34. The camp massacre took place during the Lebanese Civil War on 12 August 1976.

35. 'Ahed (2008). Personal interview with the author, Shatila Camp/Beirut: August. 'Ahed only wanted to give his first name.

36. Makrma 'Awitah (2007). Personal interview with the author, Burj al-Barajneh Camp/Beirut: April.

37. Al-Kabri was a village close to the coast, between Acre and Lebanon; it was demolished during the 1948 war (see www.palestineremembered.com).

38. Mariam Shakir Said (2007). Personal interview with the author, Wihdat Camp/Amman: April.

39. Na'ila Zayyad (2007). Personal interview with the author, Nazareth: November.

40. Political poetry in the 1950s and 1960s became a major vehicle for expressions of collective memory and resistance. Many poets, like Tawfik Zayyad, Mahmoud Darwish, Emile Habibi, Emil Touma, Samih al-Qassem and Hanna abu Hanna, were forced underground and many were kept under house arrest.
41. Bassam al-Shak'a (2007). Personal interview with the author, Nablus: November.
42. For a history of Nablus in the Ottoman period, read Beshara Doumani (1995) *Rediscovering Palestine: Merchants and Peasants in Jabal Nablus, 1700–1900*, Berkeley: University of California Press.
43. He is referring to an Israeli raid on the frontier village of Samu' on 13 November 1966, in which 118 houses were dynamited and 21 Jordanian soldiers killed. Palestinian demonstrators in several towns accused the Jordanian government of leaving them defenceless and called for the population to be armed. See Sayigh (1997) *Armed Struggle and Search for State*, p. 138.
44. Mohammed Mughrabi (2007). Personal interview, Jerusalem: November.
45. Buthaina (2008). Personal interview with the author, Yarmouk Camp/Damascus: April.

CHAPTER FIVE

Children of the Stones: Living the First *Intifada*

None of us can forget the whispers and occasional proclamations that our children are 'the population factor' – to be feared, and hence to be deported – or constitute special targets for death. I heard it said in Lebanon that Palestinian children in particular should be killed because each of them is a potential terrorist. Kill them before they kill you. (Edward Said)

By 1987, it was becoming increasingly clear that neither international powers nor Arab regimes were ready or willing to help the Palestinians living under Israeli occupation in the West Bank and Gaza Strip. The Palestinian question or Palestinian cause was last on the list of priorities at Arab summits.

The PLO's political strategy, agreed from exile in Tunis, could not come up with an immediate solution to the refugee problem or to occupation.[1] With increasingly difficult conditions for the Palestinians living under Israeli occupation in the West Bank and Gaza – routine harassment, occasional beatings, arrests without formal charges and humiliating searches by security forces at roadblocks and checkpoints– young Palestinians felt there was little to lose if they broke the rules of the game. The stage was set for the first *intifada* ('uprising' or, literally, 'shaking off').

On 8 December 1987, an Israeli truck hit two vans carrying Gaza labourers in Jabaliya, a refugee camp with 60,000 residents, killing four of them. Rumour spread that the incident was no accident, but an act of vengeance by the relative of an Israeli stabbed to death several days earlier in the Gaza market. It is not clear whether one of the first denunciatory Palestinian leaflets (*bayanat*) – later to become one of the *intifada*'s key motifs – was distributed on the same day, when thousands of mourners at the funeral of the four refugees turned on the nearby Israeli army post, assaulting it with a barrage of stones.

The *intifada* was consciously styled after, and compared with, the 1936–9 revolt. Soon, the mythic quality of the earlier revolt translated into direct and confrontational acts of resistance against Israel.[2] The uprising started in Gaza's refugee camps, where a third of the inhabitants were children under 15, and the average age, according to UNRWA, was 27.[3]

That the 1987 *intifada* was seen to be predominantly led and championed by young people, in their early to late teens, was not a new phenomenon in Palestinian history. In the first decade of the twentieth century, a group of young activists tried to advance a radical, pan-Syrian political strategy as an alternative to the narrow Palestinian nationalism espoused by their older, more conservative counterparts.[4] Later, during the British Mandate (1920–48), young men again agitated for more radical tactics in the emerging national struggle. When a fully fledged Palestinian national liberation movement emerged in the late 1960s in exile, many of its leaders were young student activists, building on the wave of Arab nationalism that swept the Middle East then.

In the 1987 *intifada,* the fighters were not professional freedom fighters, but ordinary people from all walks of life and different ages. Those who took part were young adults and teenagers carrying stones, their faces shrouded by *kuffiyehs* or masks, standing ready to confront the Israeli troops and police head on. Their message was clear: Palestinians had had enough of years of creeping annexation, a rise in the number of settlements and of the false integration of the local economy into the Israeli economy, which had created a relationship of dependence that had turned into one of the occupation's worst – and most significant – aspects. Furthermore, for two decades, the Israelis had failed to invest in Palestinian areas, instead dumping Israeli products in the occupied territories by undercutting local factories and producers. These measures were accompanied by an aggressive campaign of Hebraization of signposts in some public spaces, mirroring methods used by Israel in subjugating the Palestinian minority in Israel.

Early examples of *intifada* narratives indicate an over-whelming sense of novelty, a conviction that young people were doing something unprecedented. Some of the Palestinians I interviewed talked of the *intifada* as a turning point in their lives, an event that made them wake up to the reality of the occupation. Ishaq Abdel-Haq, from Nablus, was in his early teens at the time:

> It was only in 1987 that I realized we are under occupation. Before, I just lived my life like everyone else, going to school and playing sports. My father was working at the municipality and I did not have many problems – I mean financial ones, like many others. The *intifada* opened my eyes to the occupation, and life changed all of a sudden. By a sad coincidence, my mother had passed away six months before the *intifada* erupted. Her death was also related to the occupation. We were returning from our house in Ramallah for the weekend, when we were stopped by the Israeli soldiers. There had been a protest that day and they

threw tear gas to disperse the crowds and stop the burning tyres. I was 13 at the time. They confiscated my father's and brother's identity cards and took them to one side. My mother, who had a history of high blood pressure, stopped breathing out of worry. She died as she arrived at the hospital. I am not saying the soldiers killed her, but she died because of the occupation. I am 90 per cent certain about this.[5]

Interestingly, Palestinians inside Israel provided an unexpected source of inspiration, particularly when they reacted more swiftly than the PLO to events in the occupied territories. A few weeks after the uprising started, Palestinian activists in Israel organized strikes and demonstrations on a special day called the Day of Peace, when political action was co-ordinated by Palestinians on both sides of the Green Line.

This act of solidarity led to bolder, extended acts of resistance. An association emerged in Palestinians' minds between the *intifada* and earlier acts of land confiscation and reprisals, such as the one in the Galilee in 1976. Similar acts, on a much wider scale, brought home the nature of neo-colonialist economic dependence, symptomatic of Israel's treatment of both Palestinian communities.[6]

Ultimately, the *intifada* belonged to the Palestinian camps, mostly to those in Gaza, which housed 850,000 of the estimated combined total of 1.5 million refugees in the occupied territories at that time. The refugee camps bore the brunt of Israel's punitive measures while half of those people killed in the violence were in villages. In the first year of the *intifada*, 400 refugees were killed in clashes with the Israeli army and tens of thousands wounded, according to most sources. They were the victims of live ammunition or rubber bullets, as well as systematic beatings by Israeli soldiers and border police.

Towards the end of the *intifada* in 1991, the Israeli army imposed punitive economic controls, cutting off electricity and water and preventing olive-picking at the height of the season. Although the resemblance to the 1936–9 revolt was striking, a major difference was the involvement of women. Women from all walks of life, but particularly from rural areas, took a central role in the uprising, boldly confronting the army and forming shields to protect children. In fact, by the end of the *intifada*, a third of the overall casualties were also women,[7] yet paradoxically the uprising did not revolutionize women's lives in the sense that it did not radically change their working conditions or the occupations they chose.

One reason why the Palestinians in the West Bank and Gaza were able to persevere was the extensive experience of mass organization of Fatah, the PFLP, the DFLP and the communists, and latterly, of Islamist groups.[8] In the Gaza Strip, however, the Islamist groups – such as the Islamic Resistance Movement (*Harakat al-Muqawama al-Islamiyya*), best known by its acronym Hamas,[9] and Islamic Jihad – began to challenge the dominant world view of the various elements comprising the PLO and what was then called the Palestinian Unified Leadership, precursor of the Palestinian Authority, as well as their conceptions of who the Palestinians were and who should represent them. In the end, the uprising was not the armed rebellion that the leaders of the PLO had advocated, but a massive act of grassroots resistance. It erupted two decades after Arafat's call to arms, but was not directed by the armed resistance that he had tried to establish in previous decades.[10]

Kimmerling and Migdal (1994/2003) claim that 'de facto the intifada had created a state of stalemate, in which each side was defeated, even though neither side would admit it even to itself, and certainly not to the other.'[11] However, as subsequent events and the personal narratives below show, the *intifada* was not seen as a failure by Palestinians in Israel and the occupied territories – though it was presented in that way by the Israeli government. It was partly as a result of the *intifada* that an accord was signed six years later in Oslo – the first official, written agreement between Israel and the PLO, designed to put an end to the conflict, changing the nature of the Palestinian national struggle and its meaning.

Atfal al-Hijara ('The children of the stones')

The *muntafideen* (those who took part in the uprising or 'rebels') were Palestinians of different age groups, but it was children and teenagers who paid for their acts of resistance to Israeli occupation practices, paradoxically providing visual proof of the brutal Israeli response.

Soon, the image of 'the child of the stone' became so powerful among Palestinians that Israeli soldiers were told to direct their fire at the chief instigators – those with shrouded faces. Images of the child martyr electrified the population, leading to a new, sustained level of mobilization and revolutionary fervour. John Collins, in his engaging book about memories of the generation of the *intifada*, writes that the participants were everywhere and nowhere.

> They are almost hyper-real, making regular appearances on the evening news and on the front pages of newspapers around the world. They are on the cover of many *intifada* books, stones in hand, giving the 'V' for victory sign as they confront Israeli tanks and troops... but much like the young activists who led the protests against South Africa's apartheid regime during the 1970s and 1980s, the *atfal al-hijara* ('the children of the stones') are political caricatures about whom we know surprisingly little.[12]

Popular discourse from the early period of the *intifada* indicates that, even as these images of young Palestinian children were being beamed around the world, some people – including older Palestinians – were already asking whether the *intifada* children had been marked negatively by their experiences. In public and nationalist discourse and in other published material, writers like the late Syrian poet Nizar Qabbani depicted the young Palestinian stone throwers as larger-than-life figures single-handedly saving the national movement from stagnation, heroes standing up to Israel and the corruption of Arab leaders. Qabbani's enthusiasm for the young people's actions provoked different *intifada* narratives that spoke of the way young Palestinians, often marginalized by formal politics, were doing something unprecedented.[13] Barbara Harlow says Qabbani's poem was only the first in a long succession of odes to the 'children of the stones', many of which focused almost solely on the image of the stone.[14]

Reflections, analyses and descriptions of the *intifada* were often inflected with the language of heroism and victimization, while also suggesting that the young were more heroic for being young. Edward Said, in line with other post-colonial scholars, went further in capturing the significance of these acts as not only resisting Israeli practices, but also taking on global structures of political, economic and military domination, 'with stones and an unbent political will standing fearlessly against the blows of well-armed Israeli soldiers, backed by one of the world's mightiest defence establishments, bankrolled unflinchingly and unquestioningly by the world's wealthiest nation, supported faithfully and smilingly by a whole apparatus of intellectual lackeys.'[15]

It is fitting to end this narrative of Palestine, as a landscape and as a people, with personal stories of the *intifada*, the culmination of the first phase of the Palestinian national struggle and the first act of 'grassroots' resistance in which images of the Palestinian subject were beamed worldwide. The 'children of the stones', as they came to be known, were agents in their own story, like the *fedayeen* in the 1960s and 70s and the *mujahideen* in the 1930s. Crucially, they were the true witnesses to (as well as victims of) Israeli injustices since 1948. Images of their uprising were beamed worldwide via local and international media making thousands of others witnesses, too. The practice of Palestinians acting as witnesses to their own oppression and testifying for the benefit of outside audiences is a crucial mechanism through which the very idea of 'Palestinian-ness' begins to be visually performed and mediated and perhaps reified[16] in new ways.

This mechanism of witnessing and telling can (and does) feed into the state-building projects of the Palestinian nationalist elite, and therefore may be distorted, but it also opens questions about what Diana Allan calls the 'ethical obligation we (historians, researchers and others) have to document' and record Palestinian lives and experiences, and to reflect on the meaning of witness and the politics of what informs it.[17] As she writes,

> empathy may cause us to lose sight of distinctions – the ways in which the past does, and does not, continue to shape the present. There is clearly a need to move beyond the coercive harmony of a national identity rooted in past history to include emergent forms of subjectivity that increasingly privilege individual aspiration over collective, nationalist imperatives.[18]

One of the most potent and emotive images of the Palestinian child witness, and one that shaped the visual landscape of the uprising, is that of Handala, created by the late Palestinian political cartoonist and artist Naji al-'Ali. The symbolic figure of Handala is that of a ten-year-old boy, a figure standing alone with his back to his audience, silently witnessing a world dominated by Israeli oppression, Arab egotism and American policy-makers seeing what they want to see. The figure of Handala, whose name derives from *handhal,* a bitter plant with deep roots, was omnipresent in the camps during the *intifada,* drawn by students in their notebooks, spray-painted on walls and worn as necklaces or carried as key chains, suggesting a popularity that can be interpreted in various ways. Kamal Boullata, too, provides another example of the testimonial mode in his book *Faithful Witness,* a collection of artwork by a select group of West Bank and Gaza Palestinians, none older than fourteen, demonstrating how the image of the child as witness enables a process of humanization and normalization of Palestinians, portraying them as part of a community like any other.[19]

The first narrative in this chapter is by of a child of the stones, Mohammed Fadi Ghanayim, in which he tells evocatively of his involvement in the *intifada* and how he was shot in the leg at the age of 14. I follow this with the reflections of Amal Nashashibi, a Palestinian woman who grew up in Jerusalem and witnessed various events, including the *intifada*, and the testimony of Khaled Ziadeh, a Gazan Palestinian who witnessed at firsthand the beginning of the *intifada*. Then Manal Hazzan Abu-Sinni, a citizen of Israel brought up in Nazareth, reflects on her Palestinian-ness through her experiences of the *intifada* while in Jerusalem. I end with the recollections of Mustafa Naji al-Hazarin, a former member of Islamic Jihad, whose story raises questions about the present and how it informs the past.

I am part of this story: Mohammed Fadi Ghanayim[20]

I was born in Dheisheh Camp in Bethlehem in 1975. My first memories of my childhood are of standing in a queue, along with tens of other children, for food outside the UNRWA doors. Our situation was not so bad, however, but, like other kids in the camp, my childhood felt it was composed of a series of queues. I never asked why this had to be the case, as everyone else was doing it and I did not see what was going on outside.

As I grew older, I had questions. I began asking about the barbed wire and the tear-gas and the curfews. One day, I went with my uncle to visit his fiancée. I was seven years old. When we went in, I saw a picture of a prisoner on the wall, a man behind bars, and I asked my uncle about it. He told me it was a picture of his fiancée's brother. He was in prison because he took part in an operation against the occupation.

I remember seeing the Israeli jeeps coming into the camp and the soldiers walking about with their guns and weapons, and I used to feel I was living a historical event. Dheisheh was a hotspot for confrontation with the Israelis. In fact, to be exact, the *intifada* started in the camp in 1982. But it remained restricted to the camp. My father was forced out of his village, and it was because he was forced out that I was born and brought up in a camp. I used to think that this is a story I am part of, or am in the middle of, not the beginning of the end.

You see all these things happening on television, and you watch some dramas and soap operas, and more questions come up. As you look and think, you begin to ask why you don't have land and why did the Israelis take your land in the first place. When people say they left, it is not true. Palestinians were evicted from their land. My grandfather came with my grandmother. He left the village in 1948 and went to different places, because of what happened and because of his job. He used to move from one city to another for work so that my uncles were born in different places, one in Hebron, another in Thahryieh, a third in Akka [Acre]. He was a policeman who served under Jordan after working in the British police force during the Mandate. He ended up in Bethlehem, never able to return to his home. He had 14 children, and the family grew and grew. It is the story of many families in the camp. Imagine: it has 13,000 people living in an area of 12 sq. km [4.6 sq. ml]. I am lucky because we have managed to buy the piece of land on which I live right now.

I was 14 years old in 1987, one of those children around whom the story of this particular period revolves. I was asked to watch the street and then throw stones. I, along with some friends, felt this was the most beautiful thing to happen to us. Thinking back, it was mostly spontaneous work, with little organization. I chose to help, but I did not have any say in being shot.

I was standing in front of al-Iskandar school in Beit Jala, where I used to study. It was six in the morning and people were just getting up. They shot me in the leg with a bullet, an injury that meant I had to be treated in different hospitals for the next eight years. I had 14 operations on my leg. I was hit just below the ankle and the bullet managed to splinter the bone, eventually reducing the length of that leg by 11 cm [4 in.]. I used to dance the *dabke* and run, almost marathons, and I cannot do this any more.

I was shot by what we call a dumdum bullet, a bullet that penetrates, burns and explodes. It is forbidden under international law. Only two armies use it; one of them is the Israeli army. How do they justify this against a kid whose weapon that day was a pen, pencil and notebook? I knew I was shot because I lay there unable to get up.

That morning, I was wearing new clothes, a new pair of trousers and a new shirt with a logo. I arrived at the school with a classmate called Hassan. I could see the soldiers nearby. We did not know they would start shooting on a whim, use people as moving targets, direct their guns towards us and shoot. I only found out about this practice ten years later when I was working as a journalist writing on conflict. On that day, I clearly heard them talking among themselves, telling each other to aim at the red shirt or the yellow shirt. This is how they picked us out. Then they would decide whether it would be the leg or the hand to target.

It happened so fast. There was a spray of bullets coming from nowhere and the next thing I felt was my body on fire. I could not understand where this heat was coming from. My leg was hanging suspended in half, blood gushing like from a fountain. Nabila al-Daqaq who lived by the school, witnessed the shooting. My leg was a mixture of bones, nerves, flesh and dust from the street. I was in a state of shock and I could not figure out how to reconnect my leg to my body. I soon began to feel the cold, my teeth chattering against each other. Some students tried to take me to a nearby hospital, but the bullets came rushing by.

After they stopped shooting, which felt like it was ages, the soldiers came over to give me medical care. They took off my clothes and poured some water on the wound. I was in so much pain. I heard women shouting at the soldiers, then felt them trying to help me, pulling me one way or the other. But they could not do anything. It took three hours for an ambulance to arrive, Nabila al-Daqaq told me later.

They did not take me straight to the hospital, but to the military headquarters in Basta. I was terrified because this is where they take people before sending them to prison, and I wanted to go to hospital. They took me out of the jeep. Then a group of male and female soldiers began to take photos of me. They were not much older than me, perhaps 19. It felt as though they had caught a deer, a wolf or a rabbit, and not a human being.

One officer tried to make me sign papers to confess to what was the ultimate crime, and to sign a statement saying I was throwing stones at them. I told them in Hebrew that I had not committed any offence. All this torture was happening while the blood continued to run out of the wound. I cursed him and tore the paper in half. The soldier who attended to me first had sprayed the word 'Wanted' in Hebrew on the back of my shirt. I lay there for two more hours, refusing to sign that paper. Then I heard my mother's voice outside, screaming to be let in. She told me later that some schoolboys had taken my clothes soaked in blood to her and that she expected to see a corpse. I waved to her, and she calmed down in the knowledge I was still alive.

They brought an ambulance guarded by two soldiers, and I was taken to Hadassah Hospital in Jerusalem. There, I found most of my family waiting. In normal societies, the injured arrives in hospital before his relatives. The Israelis asked my father for money before they would operate. They wanted 37,000 shekels. He had just come in from work and did not have that money on him, so he told them to take his ID and keep it until he collected the money. He pleaded with them to operate. It was only when I went into the operating theatre that they untied me, but I heard them tell a hospital guard that this was a young 'terrorist' they were bringing in.

I was 15 years old and lucky, in that respect, because I had time on my side in terms of recovery. I shall never forget this. It was on a Wednesday, and I hate Wednesdays with a vengeance. My grandmother died on a Wednesday and my friend's house was demolished on a Wednesday. Our *Nakba* did not finish with 1948 or 1967, because we live it every day, right up to the present.

What I told you is part of my story. They continued to pressure me to sign this paper and confess. I refused. They persisted even a month after my injury and I remember throwing a glass bottle at the soldier. They refused to stop. I had 11 operations during that month, and each day I stayed at the hospital cost my family 25,000 shekels. My father was bankrupt.

It all was done in numbers. What it means to be Palestinian is to be a number; we die by numbers. There are also numbers for the wounded, for the evicted, and for the imprisoned. We are even numbers in the dictionary of nations. Today conflict revolves around checkpoints and between Hamas and Fatah. In the 1980s, there were rules and discipline. Then you have Oslo and you see the two: the killer and the killed shaking hands.

Reflections of the meaning of it all: Amal Nashashibi[21]

I was a teenager in 1967. I was living in Shu'fat near the Old City of Jerusalem. I remember my aunt's husband came to take me to their house, which is not more than half a mile from our house. We heard news on the radio that 60 planes had landed and that the Arabs were about to achieve victory. We were delirious with happiness.

The next day, bullets started to hit our house and we knew we were in the middle of the battlefield. Shu'fat was in what we might call no-man's land, subject to attacks and counter-attacks. My aunt's husband, who had lived through 1948 and knew much about war and so on, was the first to tell us that they [the Israelis] had arrived. It was only the second day of the war. We knew they had won. The next day, there were tanks on the street along with a few corpses of Jordanian soldiers left to rot in the sun. It was a landscape of defeat.

The Israelis arrived trying to make friends. They gave my mother sweets to soften her heart, but she would have none of it. Two of my brothers were studying abroad at the time, so I was the eldest of all my siblings who were there at the time. An Israeli official, not much older than I was at the time, called round to take a head count, ten days after the start of the occupation. They would count only those who were in the house at the time. We told him about my two brothers, but they refused to take notice. Those abroad do not count. They are just nothing. Overnight, we were turned from people with land to 'residents'. I remember I cried then and I remember my father holding me to comfort me.

My older brothers could not come back to Jerusalem under these new regulations, and this affected me so much. One of them, the eldest, never returned as he passed away in a car accident in Beirut. On the day of the census, I knew something deeply wrong was taking place and I knew it was the beginning of the end for Jerusalem as it had been until then. They took the surrounding hills and began to build settlements. They expelled people, randomly and with no valid reasons, and took over their homes. They emptied areas like 'Anabta and Mikmas of their residents. They continued to squeeze the population out.

We are refugees, originally refugees from West Jerusalem and all our possessions are there. Our house is on the Street of the Prophets. An eye surgeon lives there now. We went to visit the place, and he and his family opened their arms and hugged each one of us. They made us Turkish coffee. We went back again and my father asked to buy the house again, but they refused. It is clear that the Jews want to suppress our consciousness of ourselves as a people, but we are still around and our imagination remains intact.

In 1987, I was invited to Nairobi to speak at a convention for women and to present our cause. Some Palestinian feminists did not want to go, arguing that they would be sitting side by side with Jews, but I went because it is important to hear our voice. Before I went, I decided to speak to people and find out what they feel and ask them about their experiences, and it was then that I could sense something was about to take place. Young people were telling me about their grievances, about the brutality of the occupation and about being exploited in Tel Aviv and other places. They said they felt almost inhuman. I am a Palestinian woman. I have never belonged to any political faction and I never really took religion seriously, but when the *intifada* erupted, I went to the *Haram al-Sharif* [the Dome of the Rock] for the first time.

I really don't want to go into details because those days were truly horrific and people have seen it all. Thinking about it later, I started thinking that the uprising succeeded because it sprang out from within the landscape and from the people that make up Palestine. It was not planned; it was spontaneous. If it were planned, the Israelis would have found out beforehand and would have captured all the leaders, like catching birds. The *intifada* came out of suffering, and suffering was our landscape and our way of life then.

People were fed up with the treatment of workers and their [Israelis'] attitude. Sentiments reached a stage when we needed to stop the delusion that the Israelis had brought us prosperity, and accept that it was only occupation and misery. They used to say that Jerusalem was a bubble [a place apart]. There were many protests in Jerusalem, but they banned people from taking photographs or reporting. In Jerusalem, they had and still have a special force trained to beat people, literally and symbolically, into submission. There were many protests, but they would suppress these efficiently and quickly. It is still the same. Nothing has changed.

History no longer forgot the Palestinians: Khaled Ziadeh[22]

My father grew up in the camps, but moved to Gaza City at the start of 1970. I was born in Gaza City and I moved to the camp when the *intifada* started. I used to visit the Bureij Camp all the time as a child, and it was during those early years that I developed a special bond with the camp.

We became politicized, talking politics all the time because of the brutal effect of the occupation. They banned us waving the national flag, playing national music, and reading books, all of which strengthened the politicization of the community. The military government wanted us to be afraid and wanted us to forget that we had basic human rights both as individuals and also as a community and this led us to look for ways to mobilize and organize against these attempts. The local economy was almost non-existent and youths and middle-aged men had to commute and work in Israel as cheap labour. Few people had the chance to be educated. I was privileged in this respect and had the chance to go to a good school.

Before the *intifada,* it was hard to join any political faction unless this was in secret. We had limited access to published material, to books, magazines and newspapers. There were only one or two newspapers allowed, otherwise we used to read those published underground such *al-Hadaf* and *al-Jamaheer,* and some others. The political factions managed underground libraries where they tried to distribute books related to Palestine or world politics. We had access to Israeli, Egyptian and Jordanian television channels and radio stations. We used to listen to the Monte Carlo radio station, which had become popular during the *intifada* because it reported daily and extensively on the events unfolding in the West Bank and Gaza. I was obsessed with local news from Gaza, and I used to spend hours every day near *al-Shifa* hospital, the main hospital in the Gaza Strip, to find out what was going on. The occupation forces managed to make us feel non-existent in the 1970s and 1980s, and we accepted the status quo, going to work in Israel and getting on with our lives. The *intifada* made us aware that this was a mirage and that we were living in a continuous state of emergency. Their plans to convince us that they were not an occupation failed. They tried to make us turn against each other, but we got together as one community. For me, like others of the *intifada* generation, there will always be a moment in our lives that will stay with us forever and that will always be remembered as the moment that changed our lives for good. That was the *intifada.*

We decided to protest and resist the military occupation with the little means we had. Markets, shops and schools closed and crowds went on the streets in protest. Tear gas and the smoke of burning tyres changed the colour of the sky and all you heard was the sound of guns shooting live ammunition or rubber bullets that injured or killed. Taxis were used to carry the injured to local clinics. There were funerals almost every day.

It was even during these conditions that a unified leadership emerged and factions came out of hiding to mobilize the population, and the *intifada* was a mixture of organized action and spontaneous acts of resistance. The young people felt empowered and realized that history was on their side. Israel opened two new prisons, Ansar 2 and Ansar 3, to put behind bars the increasing number of detainees. Most of my friends were arrested more than once and it became clear that every young person knew he was waiting his turn to be incarcerated. The-then Israeli Defence Minister Yitzhak Rabin issued an order to break the bones of young Palestinians. They did break bones, and some days all you could see were people walking around in casts.

I decided to go to Bureij Camp on the outskirts of Gaza City when the *intifada* erupted. It was a sudden decision, because I had not planned this move beforehand. I remember that I woke up that day and felt my life had changed and had been turned completely upside down. I was 17 years old when this happened, and full of youthful energy and hope. In the camp, a daily curfew was imposed for 12 hours a day, and sometimes, in response to protests and clashes, they would impose a curfew for a week or two to exhaust the people and sap their energy. Another form of collective punishment was that they would order everyone between the age of 16 and 50 to come out of their homes and make then sit from two till six in the morning in the cold. We paid a heavy price for the uprising; unemployment rose significantly and freedom of movement restricted. Schools were out of bounds so we began informal education, at homes.

I was living alone in the camp running a grocery shop. I got injured one day and had to go for about a mile to the closest clinic during curfew time. When I returned, my hand stitched and bandaged, I was amazed to see about 25 of my neighbours waiting outside the shop to see if I needed help. This kind of support was non-existent in the city. For me, the best days of my life were those I lived in the camp. Everyone who lived and witnessed the *intifada* has a story to tell, some happy memories and some sad ones. It was wonderful to see the youth getting together and mobilizing to confront the army, and then hear them dancing the *dabke* in the streets and singing nationalist songs out in the open, unlike before when such activities were banned. Before the uprising, they banned performances of the *dabke* and you could receive a punishment of six months in prison if you defied this order. The same punishment would be given if they caught you listening to nationalist songs. During the *intifada*, the Israelis tried their best to suppress all forms of cultural performance. They did not want to catch only the stone throwers, but also those who organized, painted graffiti on walls and arranged meetings. At one point, a group of kids, not more than five years old, performed the *dabke* on the street. That's how powerful the youngsters felt.

I remember this boy who was only 13. He refused to stop throwing stones at the soldiers. It was very obvious that, despite his attempts to hit the soldiers, he could only throw his stone half-way. He was shot by a sniper whose bullet pierced his heart. For me, the *intifada* was when I began to feel what it means to be Palestinian. It is the same for all of my generation. You know, many Palestinians did not talk about the 1948 and 1967 defeats because they felt humiliated and ashamed. My grandfather did not talk about 1948 and all he talked about was the great life he lived before. My father always avoided speaking about the 1967 defeat. Both felt humiliated and ashamed. The first *intifada* changed all of that because there was something to talk about, and it was the beginning of a new generation of Palestinians that did not accept defeat.

It made us feel different: Manal Hazzan Abu-Sinni[23]

I was born in 1969 in Nazareth, where I grew up and went to school. Then I went to the Hebrew University in Jerusalem to continue my studies. I was there at the beginning of the *intifada*, studying law and working with an NGO.

7 The ongoing *Nakba.* A couple in Gaza, August 2009, standing outside the remains of their house, flattened during the 2008/9 Israeli attack. Photograph: Tanya Habjouqa.

It has always been clear to me that we, the Palestinians in Israel, are different from the rest of the people who live in this state. In Nazareth, we never felt we were a minority, because it was mainly Arab. It was only when I went to university that I felt different and I became aware that Israel was an occupation force.

There were these soldiers on the streets and they would stop us for random searches as we went around from place to place. Then they would object to us speaking in Arabic to each other. In coffee shops, frequented by Israelis, we began to understand the meaning of being a minority and the meaning of discrimination. My father used to tell us stories of relatives meeting at Mandelbaum Gate in Jerusalem after 1967. At home, our parents told us of 1948 and how the land was taken by force and the Palestinians expelled. In Jerusalem, we felt different, with a different culture, language and religion and we felt we were indeed a minority that had different rules and laws applied to it. At university, it was natural that we gravitated towards others who spoke Arabic.

The *intifada* added to the feeling of difference. There were these checkpoints, some of them randomly set up. If you looked like an Arab, with a moustache or beard, you were stopped. When we were young, we used to visit Ramallah and Bethlehem and other towns on the West Bank and think how much better they lived. When we went to the university, things changed, and these places were impossible to reach.

I remember this bus that would take us from Nazareth and Jerusalem and it would stop in Jenin and Nablus on the way. When the *intifada* started, the journey became arduous and almost impossible to do. It was the only bus to use to go to Jerusalem. One day, we passed through the Balata refugee camp. And then all of a sudden, we were stopped and the bus boarded by these Israeli soldiers. They claimed that they were after some boys throwing stones and that the boys had jumped on the bus to hide. They ordered us all out. We did not know where to go and finally they allowed us to continue the journey. It was impossible to do the route on a daily basis, so we persuaded someone to drive us by car.

I can totally understand why the Palestinians were fed up. I remember this day I was in Hebron when the Israeli soldiers began to ask for identity cards. I was terrified because I did not want them to discover I was an Arab. I sat there watching them chasing a young boy and I could not do anything. I felt angry and humiliated at the same time.

It was a difficult time because students were arrested at protests we organized at the university. Others were arrested in Nazareth. On Land Day and on the anniversary of the massacre of Sabra and Shatila, a strike was called, but some teachers were worried about taking part for fear of dismissal. My brother would not allow me to join the protests against the Israeli invasion of Lebanon, but I wrote in my diary how the soldiers beat the protestors and how some escaped and came to hide in our house. They are funny things, diaries, because mine is a mixture of the many aspects of my life as a girl and a teenager, but also of everyday politics.

Politics was at the centre of our lives at home and at school, without us knowing it. My father was a teacher and they [my parents] never had much money and sometimes he did not get any salary, but he continued to teach. I never really separated from other Palestinians, but there was something about my time in Jerusalem that made me feel my Palestinian-ness much more. In Jerusalem, I began to exist as myself.

Ask Hamas: Mustafa Naji al-Hazzarin[24]

I am the son of refugees, born in the Shuja'iya Camp in Gaza in 1966. I grew up with stories of Palestine, of the *fedayeen*, the beginning of the Palestinian resistance movement and the hope of liberation.

In reality, my main concern in those early years was education. I loved school. I used to walk to school, though it would take me an hour to get there, and run on my way back home to catch the evening news on the radio. People used to encourage their children to study science, to become doctors or engineers. I wanted to be a politician and wanted to study politics. My father thought I was mad when I told him my intentions. My mother laughed: '*Oof ya ibni!* (Oh my son!) How can you become a diplomat when we have no state?'

I think what changed me was the 1982 invasion of Lebanon. In those days, many young people were attracted to the Muslim Brotherhood movement. One of my teachers was an avid supporter of the movement, talking about Islam with such tenderness and warmth that we could not but be affected by the depth of his belief. Even before the invasion, there were many young people who adopted an Islamic ideology that perceived Palestine as an Islamic entity. We were young and impressionable and were very taken by the idea that Islam was our route out of our misery. And this idea and what it stood for was refreshingly honest, unlike what Fatah would have made us believe.

I became active, taking part in meetings and protests. When one of the teachers, who belonged to Islamic Jihad, was fired from the Islamic University and lost his job, I went with a group of sympathizers to protest against this action. When my father found out I had been involved in these protests, he threw me out of the house. I went to my uncle's house. Those were difficult times because the Israeli intelligence service had already found out about me and they put me under house arrest.

I was under house arrest for a year, between 1982 and 1983, a whole year I spent going to report to the civil administration's headquarters from morning till night. I used to sit from seven in the morning till seven in the evening, giving them my identity card in the morning so I would not be able to go anywhere and taking it back in the evening when they allowed me to go back. They used cunning techniques to stop us learning. They knew how to torture you psychologically while taking exams. For instance, they would allow you to sit an exam on the first day, but arrest you on the second, or they would take you in the morning and release you in the evening. Hundreds missed their exams, and failed, because of this.

I come from a big family of 12 children. Our socio-economic situation was good compared to others. My father was a businessman and my mother a seamstress. All they talked about was Palestine. My mother would always say she felt sorry for Yasser Arafat because he had to move from one place to another, with no stable sanctuary. At least, she would say, we were in our own home. I won't go into many details because I have so many memories and stories to tell and that would mean talking for days.

I was accepted at Cairo University when I achieved the highest grades at my school and scored the fourth highest in the whole of Gaza. The Egyptians would not accept me or allow me to enter the country. I applied to study English literature in Pakistan, but my father prevented me from going. I went on strike, refusing to do anything much but go to meetings. After two years, I changed my mind and applied to study at al-Najah University in Nablus. Nablus in those days attracted many supporters of the Popular Front for the Liberation of Palestine, with whom I used to have heated arguments. But most were very open to discussions and stuck with their principles, unlike Fatah people. I was already with Islamic Jihad.

Then the news came that I had a place at Birzeit University, and I felt that I was finally going to be able to make up for the lost years. There, my ties with Islamic Jihad grew stronger, but the Israelis knew everything about me. I remember the day I went back to Gaza and was having my hair cut. When I went home, I could not find my books. My mother told me she had hidden them underground because the Israeli army was searching for Islamic Jihad members.

I knew the time of real struggle had begun. And that was how it started. People came out in large numbers, without any prompting, to confront the occupiers. It was a time of hope. And it was this hope that made me leave Birzeit and enrol at the Islamic University in Gaza just before the *intifada* started.

I used to distribute communiqués [*bayanat*] and had little sleep in those days. Islamic Jihad had a detailed programme for confronting the Israelis. Theirs was the language of political Islam, but this was not a divisive language. It was not abstract either, but had specific meanings and contexts. The aim was clear; there was a need to bring Islam back in. Things had started to unravel when Palestine was divorced from its Arab Islamic context.

My activities were soon ended when I was imprisoned in 1989 for six months. This was called an administrative detention. Gaza was divided into small areas, each governed by a security branch. The officers could imprison you without reason. Six months could extend to ten years. I was lucky. But they jailed me at a critical time. It was a time when the *intifada* had disintegrated, when people were being assassinated because of allegations that they had collaborated with the Israelis. It was the beginning of the phenomenon of the masked men on the streets, which continues to this day, and those were frightening times. Everyone knew that if a masked man were to visit your home, then you would be branded as a collaborator.

In prison, we read a lot, and we had hopes that things would be better when we got out, but it was the same because when I came out of prison there were so many factions trying to get recruits, all at the expense of the people, the grassroots, who started the *intifada*.

I was imprisoned because someone told on me. This means you are guilty even if you are not. It is a law Israel uses to keep people incarcerated.

They came for me at 10 o'clock at night. A curfew was in place from dusk to dawn. My mother had gone during the day to the market in Lydd and had come back with a sweater for me to wear. I was sitting down for a meal of kebab, which I was enjoying while reading a book called *The Second Islamic Internationalism* by Abu al-Qassim. It was difficult for me then because I could not understand the discourse. I can now. My younger brother Fady was at home. He had gone to my grandfather's house and had come back with a small black dog. When my mother saw it, she told him it was bad luck and that she did not like black dogs. He had begged her to keep it all day and she told him he should ask me when I came back. So when I arrived home, Fady started kissing my hands and pleading with me to allow him to keep the dog. I did not mind.

That same night, the dog started barking as though terrified. My mother looked out of the window. In fright and her face white, she told us there were many Israeli soldiers in the grove, their guns pointing at the dog. Things happened fast, and the next thing I know is that they came in and asked my father about his sons, then asked him to count them by name from the eldest to the youngest. They stopped him when he said my name. I knew what was going to happen. As they took me, my mother shouted: 'Where are you taking him?'

They asked me to put my head down and walk with my head bent through the groves. It was pitch black and gloomy, and all you could hear were some people talking through their walky-talkies. It was like a scene from a film, almost surreal. We walked along, some of them kicking me, punching me and asking me whether I spoke any Hebrew. I lied and said I did not. I could hear them telling each other that they had grabbed a member of Islamic Jihad. They tied my hands and threw me in a jeep, then stamped their heavy boots on me.

The jeep zigzagged through the small streets until we reached where they were taking me. They asked me to get out, but I could not, because I was tied up like a sack. One of them grabbed me and threw me on the street. I thought that was the end of me because I could not remember much else. Then, when I did, someone was leaning over me telling me he was a doctor and that he wanted to examine my head. I went into a dream of death.

When I regained consciousness, I began to think that I would be lucky to die this way. I felt pressure in my ears and touched them, and realized I was bleeding. My mouth tasted of blood too. A group of soldiers came and put me on a stretcher then took me in an ambulance. My brain was telling me to escape, but I could not. I felt so tired. They took me to the hospital in Askelon in Israel. A doctor asked who did this to me. I could not see him, but his accent suggested he was an Arab. Perhaps he was an Arab from Nazareth.

When I improved, they took me back to the first station where I had been taken when arrested, beating me all the way. I felt abandoned, guilty, shamed, a mixture of feelings that I could not make any sense of. They eventually released me and I had to make my way back to the camp, which was under siege at the time. I arrived at my home and my father took me to see a specialist, who said there was no more danger. Five days later, they came again and took me.

I still feel confused talking about this because I cannot remember the exact chronological details of events. But the last thing I remember of the interrogation was one of them asking me about a statement Hamas had sprayed on a wall. It said: 'The *intifada* will continue until all soldiers withdraw from our lands.' The officer asked me to read this in Arabic and I did. He asked me whether I believed it, and I said that these were not my words. He then said: 'Okay then, if we leave Gaza and the West Bank, okay. But do you think we will leave Haifa and Jaffa? And where shall we go to?' I replied: 'I don't know. Ask Hamas.'

8 A woman and infant girl walk past construction rubble in the Abed Rabbo area in Gaza. Photograph: Tanya Habjouqa.

Notes

1. Ilan Pappé (2006) *A History of Modern Palestine*, Cambridge: Cambridge University Press.
2. Baruch Kimmerling and Joel S. Migdal (2003) *The Palestinian People: A History*, Cambridge, MA: Harvard University Press, p. 297.
3. Pappé (2006) *A History of Modern Palestine*, p. 231.
4. John Collins (2004) *Occupied by Memory: The Intifada Generation and the Palestinian State of Emergency*, New York: New York University Press, p. 18.
5. Ishaq Abdel-Haq (2007). Personal interview with the author, Nablus: November.
6. Pappé (2006) *A History of Modern Palestine*, p. 235.
7. Ibid., p. 236.
8. Yezid Sayigh (1997) *Armed Struggle and the Search for State*, Oxford: Oxford University Press, p. 689.
9. Hamas is an offshoot of the Muslim Brotherhood movement in Egypt. Like its Arab counterparts, the Palestinian branch took heart from the defeat of 1976, seeing it as proof of the failure of secular socialism and nationalism. Its representative in Gaza was Ahmed Yassin, a refugee born in 1938, who became a

preacher after poverty and a crippling accident had prevented his attendance at university. He was assassinated by Israeli forces in 2004.

10. Kimmerling and Migdal (2003) *The Palestinian People*, p. 286.
11. Ibid., p. 236.
12. John Collins (2004) *Occupied by Memory*, p. 11.
13. Ibid., p. 41.
14. Barbara Harlow (1989) 'Narrative in prison: stories from the Palestinian *intifada*', *Modern Fiction Studies* 35/1, pp. 29–46.
15. Edward Said (1989) '*Intifada* and independence' in Zachary Lockman and Joel Beinin (eds) *Intifada: The Palestinian Uprising against Israeli Occupation*, Boston: South End Press, pp. 5–22.
16. John Collins (2004) *Occupied by Memory*, p. 67.
17. Diana Allan (2007) 'The politics of witness: remembering and forgetting 1948 in Shatila Camp' in Ahmad Sa'di and Lila Abu-Lughod, (eds) (2007) *Nakba: Palestine, 1948, and the Claims of Memory*, New York: Columbia University Press, p. 277.
18. Ibid., p. 277.
19. Kamal Boullata (1990). *Faithful Witnesses: Palestinian Children Recreate Their World.* New York: Olive Branch Press.
20. Mohammed Fadi Ghanayim (2007). Personal interview with the author, Doha/Beit Jala: November.
21. Amal Nashashibi (2007). Personal interview with the author, Beit Jala: April.
22. Khaled Ziadeh (2007). Personal Interview with the author, London: March. Khaled is the only Gazan I interviewed outside of Gaza or the geographical area I chose to work in because of the lack of access.
23. Manal Hazzan Abu Sinni (2007). Personal interview with the author, Nazareth: November.
24. Mustafa Naji al-Hazzarin (2008). Personal interview with the author, Beirut/ August.

EPILOGUE

We used to have checkpoints in the past, but now we have the wall and it is impossible to go to Jerusalem or other places to work, so I go over to Jerusalem under cover of the dark night with some 10 women or so. We clamber over hills and step over stones. We fall and bruise ourselves, but there is no time to nurse our wounds. We have to get there before the Israeli soldiers get us and send us back. I am 64, a mother and grandmother, but I have to endure this to earn a few dollars to support my daughter and her children. With the current conditions, the closures, the checkpoints, the inability for people in the Palestinian Territories to go to other areas, or Jerusalem, our men folk have little chance of finding proper jobs. It is hard. I am not afraid as the worst that could happen to me is to die. I carry a small bag with water, a piece of bread and an apple, on my night journey, every Wednesday night. I wear a long black coat so as not to be detected. I was once caught and I tried to joke with the Israeli soldier, who was not much older than my grandson, telling him I could be his grandmother and that I mean no harm. He made me turn back. This is our life these days. 'The strong eats the weak' (al-qawi ya'kul al'da'if) in these conditions. We just want to live. (Um Khaled, Beit Jala)

I was 26 years old when I told anyone I was Palestinian. I did not know anything about our history because my parents did not talk about it. I only knew that I was different from my Lebanese friends when I was in my twenties though we did speak in a different dialect at home. I live in Antelyas, a predominantly Christian Lebanese area dominated by supporters of the right-wing Phalange Party. I was born in 1973 in Lebanon and I have a Lebanese passport. I went to good schools and university here. I am conscious my parents did a lot for us, but I am also conscious they made us hide our identity. My father was born in Haifa, but never told us about his departure from his or why he left. He told me his story when I began asking questions. I told my boyfriend I was Palestinian, and the act of telling took me four hours. I knew he would understand and would not shun me, or look down on me, but still it took me four hours to tell him who I was. These days I think about this a lot and I think that what it means to be Palestinian is a constant identity crisis. Most Palestinians feel the same way and have the same angst. We look at the map and there is nothing called Palestine. It does not exist. All we see is a map of Israel and the Occupied Territories. It is difficult to tell people who you are as much as it is difficult to tell the Palestinians in the refugee camps where I sometimes work as a volunteer that I have Lebanese citizenship. I feel guilty because I have this privilege. Does citizenship give you an identity? Am I Lebanese then? It is difficult to answer this question as much as it is difficult to understand how we, I mean my family, ended up here and not there. My sister and I keep having arguments about this. She brings her children up as Lebanese and does not see a problem with this. I do not have children and I wonder what I will do when I do have children. Sometimes when I tell people that I am Palestinian, some are surprised and some ask me: 'Really, you do not look Palestinian!' So how does a Palestinian look? Are we not human? (Dalia, Beirut)

I live in Nazareth in Israel, but I grew up an Arab. Some of my friends who grew up with me say they are Israeli, but they never learnt about their history. I lived with stories about Palestine, about 1948 and after. Now, of course, I watch the news and search the Internet and I learn all the time. I do the same things as others here, go to the cinema, buy clothes from the same malls as Israelis and even go to their universities. I am currently in my last year at the Hebrew University in Jerusalem. It is not easy to get a good education and Arab students like myself have to work hard to compete for places. Who says we are equal citizens? I speak their language, Hebrew, but I grew up speaking

Arabic at home. On the outside, it seems things are fine and
we co-exist, but things are not fine. We talk politics at home
all the time and we know things are not fine. I remember
watching the events of the second *intifada* on television and
feeling angry. I wanted to do something. A demonstration
took place in Nazareth, but I was too young and I stayed at
home. (Jita, Nazareth)

Besides its domestic impact, the first *intifada* started a process
of change at the regional level. In July 1988, King Hussein
of Jordan, which had ruled the West Bank from 1948 until
1967, announced that his country was renouncing its claims to
the territory, easing the long-standing rivalry between Jordan
and the PLO over who represented the Palestinians and paving
the way for a diplomatic initiative by the Palestinian leadership-
in-exile.

At a meeting in Algiers in November 1988, the Palestine
National Council (PNC), the PLO's parliament-in-exile,
produced two important documents: a Declaration of
Independence and a political communiqué. The declaration,
ostensibly aimed at redirecting the Palestinian *intifada* towards
a different agenda,[1] recognized the partition of Palestine both
as a crime against the Palestinian people and as a necessity to
end the conflict with Israel. Both documents opened the door
for an unprecedented public dialogue with the United States.
Both were condemned by Hamas (*Harakat al-Muqawama
al-Islamiyya*) which had emerged in the late 1980s as an Islamist
and nationalist alternative to the PLO[2] and within two decades
had transformed itself into a key political actor, though it
continued to be branded as a terrorist organization by the
United States and Israel.[3]

A number of important domestic developments had helped
facilitate negotiations between Israel and the PLO. These

9 Life goes on. Palestinian women out on a sea excursion along the Gaza coast.
Photograph: Tanya Habjouqa.

included the PLO's 1988 decision to declare a state in Gaza
and the West Bank (thereby accepting a two-state solution),
the endorsement in Israel of the idea of unilateral withdrawal
from the densely populated Gaza Strip, the 1992 election of
an Israeli Labour government (which replaced the hard-line
government of Yitzhak Shamir) and frustration with ongoing
negotiations in Washington under the Madrid Conference
framework. This framework was developed at the 1991 Madrid
Conference, a largely symbolic forum that was arguably doomed
by the refusal of the right-wing Israeli government to talk to PLO
representatives.

In the end, it was the Norwegian-brokered 'back-channel'
negotiations – between the PLO and Israelis affiliated to
the Labour-led government of Yitzhak Rabin, in power in
mid-1992 – that led to mutual Israel–PLO recognition, the
subsequent Oslo Accords and the creation of the Palestinian
authority. News that the two sides had met in secret and agreed
on a framework for future negotiations that would end their

conflict was met with heightened anticipation and extraordinary optimism in the region and beyond. However, Yasser Arafat's opting for the open-ended Oslo agreement and his historic handshake with Israeli Prime Minister Yitzhak Rabin at the White House in Washington on 13 September 1993 were seen as the manoeuvres of a politician keen to survive and assume the trappings of statehood.

The signing of what was officially called the Declaration of Principles was a far cry from the PLO's original goal of the 'total liberation' of Mandate Palestine, and a much-reduced independent state from the one envisaged by the PNC in November 1988. The main criticism was that the PLO leadership had relinquished the right to an independent state by failing to obtain specific Israeli agreement that this option would remain open at the end of the interim period.[4] This criticism was not without substance. The Israeli prime minister, Yitzhak Rabin, approved the draft only after concluding that the PLO was 'on the ropes' and would be amenable to Israeli conditions,[5] though he felt it was necessary to recognize the PLO and acknowledge the 'legitimate rights of the Palestinian people'.[6]

The Oslo agreement was devised by Israelis of the Zionist left, keen to seek an agreement with the PLO based on a solution acceptable to the Zionist parties excluded from the Labour-led government.[7] Although the PLO leadership was aware of these limitations, it considered it had no choice but to accept them.[8] In fact, it argued that the new Palestinian Authority's possession of a distinct, if limited, territorial, administrative and revenue base, and its ability to construct stable new political structures and social alliances, enhanced its international standing, helping to mobilize diplomatic support and funding.

However, a truncated, divided Palestinian state was not what the Palestinian people had struggled for and the Oslo agreement was widely viewed as merely a diplomatic cover for additional Israeli territorial expansionism under peaceful conditions. Intellectuals like the late Edward Said argued that no degree of independence or liberation could be meaningful without removing the legal, social and economic disabilities that set the Palestinians apart and divided them into three segments: those in the occupied territories of the West Bank, Gaza and East Jerusalem; those inside Israel; and the exiles.[9] To change this would require a determined, systematic and protracted struggle combining all these segments and joining with those Israeli Jews who did not want to control another people, nor privilege an apartheid system denying the existence of the natives of the land or wanting their departure.

Hamas was unequivocally opposed to the agreement, but its relationship with the Palestinian Authority was more complex. Indeed, Hamas was divided into two camps: those who favoured, at least in the early stages, integration with Yasser Arafat's regime; and those who advocated sticking with the traditional goals of holy war (*jihad*) against Israel, the liberation of the holy land and, only then, the establishment of a theocratic Islamic state.[10]

The desire to reconnect with the past and with religious codes of conduct was not limited to Muslims, but was also evident in the Jewish community within Israel. This desire proved to be a resilient and adaptive force that provided justification for extreme forms of political activity on both sides. Palestinian youth were ready to become human bombs – starting the cult of the 'suicide bomber' – and zealous Jewish settlers were willing to kill their Palestinian neighbours.[11] One such settler assassinated Israeli Prime Minister Yitzhak Rabin in November 1995.

Arafat's arrival in the occupied territories in July 1994 to take direct control of the newly established Palestinian Authority marked the end of a distinctive period that began with the Palestinians' collective dispossession and dispersal in 1948. The evolution of the PLO from a national movement in exile to a governmental apparatus on Palestinian soil signalled a shift away from the nature and form of Palestinian politics as it had evolved in the intervening years, and which the narratives in this book reminisce about.[12] Another fundamental change was the shift away from the discourse of total liberation and the top-down strategies of the armed struggle as various local and international considerations, including the eventual collapse of the first *intifada,* simple fatigue, inter-factional differences and the 1991 Gulf War came into play.

Yezid Sayigh writes that the evolution of the Palestinian armed struggle was determined by three main factors: first, the complex relationship between the Palestinians and the Arab host societies, since the leadership and the main body of the PLO were based in exile; second, the division between 'inside' and 'outside', especially after the 1967 war when Israel seized control of the rest of Mandate Palestine; and third, the nature of the Palestinian leadership and its politics.[13] Interestingly, the crucial formative experiences for the entire generation who took control of the PLO were the catastrophe of 1948, which the future leaders witnessed firsthand as teenagers or young men, and their lives under the authority of various Arab states. Although the nature of the struggle changed after Oslo, the conflict with Zionism remained unresolved and the consequences of the *Nakba* were not addressed.

Following Oslo, the change in the balance of power in favour of Israel translated into a brutal reality on the ground, manifested in all spheres of Palestinian life. In fact, despite Oslo, Israel's grip on the occupied territories tightened through its use of violent and intimidating practices, such as arrest, detention and house demolition. Its settlement plans continued unchecked. The Israeli Labour government invested 46 million dollars in the Jewish settler population of about 144,000 in the occupied Palestinian territories, much more than its Likud predecessors. By 1996, the settler population had increased by 48 per cent in the West Bank and by 62 per cent in the Gaza Strip.[14]

Israel built a series of bypasses and tunnels, dividing up the territories and creating a real and an imagined map of a Jewish West Bank imposed on the Palestinian one. Small Jewish settlements were connected to larger ones and to Israel proper by highways. The Palestinians living in the area were squeezed in and encircled by these settlements so they could move around only by passing through a series of military barriers with extreme difficulty. Ilan Pappé, the revisionist historian who used the term 'ethnic cleansing' to describe the detailed Zionist plans to evict Palestinians from their villages and towns in 1948, wryly dubbed the paving of highways, the digging of tunnels and the cantonization of the West Bank, the 'Oslo Process'.[15] With Palestinians finding it difficult to move even from one part of the West Bank to the other, and amid the brutality of the Israeli soldiers and policemen manning the checkpoints leading to Israeli areas, reality finally overtook the image that political leaders had created around the Oslo process. After 1996, the question was no longer whether Oslo had brought peace between Israel and the Palestinians, but rather what price people had paid for these illusions.[16]

Though the peace negotiations that started in Madrid in 1991 continued until the Camp David summit in July 2000, no progress was made on the key issues that separated the two sides. The impasse was inevitable given the nature of the ground rules for the negotiations, imposed by the United States under Israeli insistence: final-status issues (occupation, settlements, Jerusalem, refugees and permanent borders) were put on hold, but there was no freeze on the building of settlements in the West Bank and East Jerusalem, leading to a rise in the number of settlers from 200,000 to over 400,000 during that period. In over nine years of negotiations, the

Palestinians were barred from discussing any of the real problems, including the question of the refugees. Occupation continued, as did seizures of Palestinian land.

By the start of the second *intifada* (the al-Aqsa *Intifada*) in 2000, the Oslo peace process was already dead; even many Israelis felt it had failed to protect their personal security.[17] The second *intifada* began in October 2000, after Ariel Sharon's provocative walk through Haram al-Sharif on 28 September, escorted by hundreds of Israeli riot police.[18] The ingredients for an explosion were present even before that, but Sharon's visit threw a match onto a powder trail laid down by the failure of Oslo.

The second *intifada* belonged not only to Hamas or the refugee camps, but also to a new generation of grassroots activists that had emerged in the occupied territories. This generation was the home-grown Young Guard of Fatah which predominated in the West Bank. It was personified by Marwan Barghouti, the young Fatah activist who entered the fray as a teenager and rose to a leadership position in the first *intifada*. He returned from exile in Jordan in 1994 committed to creating an independent Palestine, but his quest ended in a collision with Arafat over reforms, institution-building and the strengthening civil society. He is currently serving a life sentence in an Israeli prison for what Israel says are terrorist offences.

The uprising followed the collapse of the peace summit at Camp David convened in July 2000 by US President Bill Clinton, and bringing together Ehud Barak, prime minister of Israel, and Yasser Arafat, chairman of the Palestinian Authority (PA). Each side blamed the other for the failure, but the obstacles to agreement were already there and many, including territorial disputes, the status of Jerusalem (which both sides claimed as their national capital), the status of refugees and Israeli security concerns. As a result, Arafat postponed the declaration of statehood for an independent Palestinian state planned for 13 September 2000.

Unlike the first *intifada,* when protests against Israeli occupation were widespread across towns and cities, this time the clashes occurred primarily on the borders of towns, on bypass roads and at Israeli-controlled religious sites. Within months, Israel exploited the presence of armed Palestinian police and security forces to justify its use of more extensive military force, despite the fact that PA forces were not initially involved in the uprising.[19]

As Palestinian resistance grew more militarized and Israeli attacks more deadly, Palestinian–Israeli violence rose to a level unparalleled since the 1982 Israeli invasion of Lebanon, punctuated by horrific scenes of suicide bombings against Israelis, Israeli aerial bombardment, military incursions into camps (including the incursion into Jenin camp in April 2000) and the use of tanks and artillery in heavily built-up areas. A new Palestinian hero, the *shahid* ('martyr') or suicide bomber, became the latest cultural symbol in the national struggle, raising the profile and appeal of the Islamic resistance movement, led by Hamas.

The unrestrained violence in Israel's reconquest of the West Bank in 2002 – the destruction of Palestine's incipient institutions, the trashing of the databases of the Palestinian education ministry, the siege of Arafat's compound in Ramallah that confined the PLO leader to four rooms in a ruin – was meant to send a message: Israel was interested only in the Palestinians' capitulation. In the three years from June 2001, all the Palestinian groups called four ceasefires, and all were ignored by Israel. In that period, Israel killed about 350 Palestinians and assassinated 21 of their leaders in 'targeted killings', including of Sheikh Ahmed Yassin, Hamas' spiritual leader, and Abdel Aziz al-Rantisi, its political leader in Gaza.[20]

The popular uprising quickly developed into a full-scale inter-communal war that blurred the distinction between civilians and fighters. During this period, nearly 5,000 people were killed in Palestine/Israel and about 35,000 were wounded. Almost 80 per cent of those killed and an even higher proportion of those wounded were Palestinians, with the majority on both sides being civilians. Thousands of Palestinians were imprisoned, and in 2002 Israeli forces began reoccupying the cities, towns and villages they had evacuated after the Oslo Accords.

Yasser Arafat died of natural causes in Paris on 11 November 2004, closing a lengthy chapter in modern Palestinian politics. His death came at a time when Palestinians faced a reinforced occupation and decades-long dispersal, while confronting a cohesive US–Israeli alliance and suffering from a nearly century-old tradition of weak self-governance and disunity.

To Arafat, and to his fellow founders of Fatah, goes much of the credit for reviving the Palestinian cause in the first two decades after 1948, but to him and his aides also belongs a share of the blame for the problems with which his people were saddled at his death. This is particularly true, as Rashid Khalidi says, of the flaws in the political structures that developed during his era of dominance.[21] Arafat's passing inspired strong positive and negative feelings among the Palestinian people and other Arabs, eliciting intense mourning alongside veiled relief and bringing to the surface a sense of anxiety at the death of the only leader most Palestinians had ever known.

Mahmoud Abbas was elected PA president in January 2005, on a platform of continuing peaceful negotiations with Israel and non-violent tactics to achieve Palestinian objectives. In August 2005, the-then Israeli Prime Minister Ariel Sharon, ordered the eviction of all Israelis from the Gaza Strip and from four settlements in the northern West Bank. At the same time, Israel tightened its grip on the West Bank, eventually illegally annexing a further 10 per cent of the land under cover of building what it called a 'security' barrier. This barrier, referred to by Palestinians and others as the 'apartheid wall', was built almost entirely within the West Bank, separating communities and sowing more resentment and anger.[22]

In January 2006, despite Israeli, US and other Western attempts to isolate it as an alleged terrorist group, Hamas won a landslide victory in the second Palestinian Legislature elections, sweeping aside Fatah's monopoly on power and undermining the hegemony of the PA inside the occupied territories and its efforts to co-opt or incorporate Hamas and its smaller Islamist rival, Islamic Jihad. Most important, Fatah lost its legitimacy and credibility because of its inability to play a more assertive role in negotiations with the Israelis.

The elections, declared fair and transparent by independent international monitors, heralded a new phase in the history of Palestinian politics, which until then had been dominated by secular nationalism. Hamas won some extra votes for its wide-ranging social programmes aimed at helping ordinary people, but its increased support was attributed to its successful appropriation of the language of Palestinian national liberation, originally devised by the secular factions in the 1960s and 1970, but gradually dropped by Fatah and PA elites as they became more comfortable with the language of the so-called peace process.[23]

The election results were rejected by Israel, the US, the EU and Russia, all citing the refusal of Hamas to accept three preconditions: to recognize Israel, to renounce violence, and to accept the validity of all previous agreements between Israel, the PLO and the Palestinian Authority. Boycotting Hamas while supporting the democratic process has been self-defeating because it failed to exploit the Islamists' desire for legitimacy and recognition while exposing the West to the charge of double standards.

Furthermore, as David Gardner writes, there is no legal or moral reason why Hamas should recognize a state that refuses to define its own boundaries. Hamas can make the point that the right to resist foreign occupation is enshrined in the UN charter (though it is also a cornerstone of international law that combatants should not target civilians) and can argue that recognizing past agreements is a moot point. With the Israeli government trampling over so many of its obligations under Oslo, it is hard to know what these mean.[24]

The elections results divided the occupied territories into an isolated, Hamas-controlled Gaza Strip and a West Bank controlled by the Palestinian Authority and its president, Mahmoud Abbas, with the support of the international community.[25] The situation has brought an escalation in the war of words and armed conflict between the two factions. In June 2007, the short-lived Fatah–Hamas national unity government collapsed, leading to violent clashes between Fatah and Hamas supporters.

In September 2007, citing an intensification of Qassam rocket attacks by Hamas, Israel declared Gaza 'hostile territory' and imposed a blockade, preventing the transport of electricity, fuel and other supplies into the territory. The stated purpose of this blockade, widely condemned as collective punishment, was to pressure Hamas into ending rocket attacks and to deprive it of the supplies needed to carry out the attacks.

On 24 December 2008, Israel launched a massive three-week offensive in the Hamas-ruled Gaza Strip. More than 1,400 people (including 926 civilians) were killed in Operation Cast Lead. Thousands more were injured and hundreds of thousands were forced to leave their homes, according to a Palestinian rights group. Thirteen Israelis were killed. The aerial bombardments and ground invasion were carefully planned, although Israel claimed that Hamas had broken a six-month ceasefire.

In March 2009, after winning parliamentary approval for his right-leaning government, Benjamin Netanyahu was sworn in as Israeli prime minister, returning to power ten years after he was voted out. Meanwhile, Arab efforts to reconcile Fatah and Hamas led to nowhere, leaving the 5 million Palestinians living in the former mandatory Palestine and the 4–6 million outside (reliable figures are not available) with no clear direction – neither clear, accepted leadership, nor a clear, acceptable basis for political progress.

Notes

1. Ilan Pappé (2006) *A History of Modern Palestine*, Cambridge: Cambridge University Press, p. 239.
2. Baruch Kimmerling and Joel S. Migdal (2003) *The Palestinian People: A History*, p. 369.
3. The movement emerged amid an increasing Islamization trend in the Arab world and deepening disillusionment with the Palestinian secular movements and their overtures to Israel.
4. Yezid Sayigh (1997) *Armed Struggle and Search for State*, Oxford: Oxford University Press, p. 659.
5. Ibid.
6. This position was due to several factors, not least the *intifada*, which had driven home the lessons that Israel could neither ignore Palestinian nationalism nor defeat it indefinitely and that the 'Jordanian option' (proposing Jordan as homeland to the Palestinians) was no longer a viable means to contain it. Israel could not incorporate the Palestinians fully in its own political and civic system without undermining its character as a Jewish state, a concern it still has today. See Sayigh (1997) *Armed Struggle and Search for State.*
7. Pappé (2006) *A History of Modern Palestine*, p. 240.
8. Following the Gulf War, the position of the PLO had been weakened and the standing of its key leaders dented. Yet Arafat felt that the key element of the accord was that it extended formal Israeli recognition of the PLO and ensured the transfer of its state-in-exile to the occupied territories.
9. Naseer H. Aruri (2005) 'Foreword' in Nur Masalha (ed.) *Catastrophe Remembered: Palestine, Israel and the Internal Refugees*, London: Zed Books.
10. Kimmerling and Migdal (2003) *The Palestinian People*, p. 369.
11. Pappé (2006) *A History of Modern Palestine*, p. 246.
12. This shift does not deny that the state-political system that had developed in exile had reproduced itself in the occupied territories.
13. Sayigh (1997) *Armed Struggle and the Search for State*, pp. 675–7.
14. Pappé (2006) *A History of Modern Palestine*, p. 243.
15. Ibid., p. 243.
16. Ibid., p. 245.

17. Ibid., p. 272.
18. Kimmerling and Migdal (2003) *The Palestinian People*, p. 392.
19. Rema Hammami and Salim Tamari (2001) 'The second uprising: end or new beginning?' *Journal of Palestine Studies*, Vol. 30, pp. 5–25.
20. In September 1997, Israel attempted to assassinate Hamas leader Khaled Mesha'al in Amman, three days after King Hussein communicated to Israel a Hamas offer of a 30-year truce. See Avi Shlaim (2007) *Lion of Jordan*, London: Allen Lane, pp. 570–76.
21. Rashid Khalidi (2006) *The Iron Cage: The Story of the Palestinian Struggle for Statehood*, Oxford: Oneworld Publications, p. 142.
22. Ibid., p. 205.
23. Saree Makdisi (2008) *Palestine Inside Out: An Everyday Occupation*, New York: W.W. Norton, p. 271.
24. David Gardner (2009) *Last Chance: The Middle East in the Balance*, London: I.B.Tauris, pp. 197–8.
25. The United States channelled funds to Fatah, while Israel allowed huge quantities of weapons and ammunition to get through to both official and unofficial Fatah militias, to destabilize Hamas.

GLOSSARY

al-Nakba	'the catastrophe' – the Zionist expulsion of Palestinian Arabs, 1948
al-Naksa	'the setback' – the Israeli take-over of the West Bank, 1967
al-thawra	'the revolution' – Palestinian armed rebellion, 1969–82
al-thawra al-kubra	'the great revolt' – Palestinian armed rebellion, 1936–9
bunduqiya	gun
Dabke	a form of dance
fedayee(n)	'guerrillas(s)' – armed civilian in a rebellion (1960s/1970s)
hamula	clan
Haram al-Sharif	the Dome of the Rock, site of al-Aqsa Mosque
Harakat al-Qaymiyyun al-'Arab	Arab Nationalist Movement
hijrah 'migration'	the flight of Palestinian Arabs in 1948
intifada	'shaking off' – civil insurrection, 1987–91
Laje'een	refugees
Masabeeh	lamps

mujahidee(n) 'guerrilla(s)'	member of a militia in a *jihad* or righteous war
mukhtar	head of the village (clan)
natour	guard
Naziheen	displaced Palestinians following 1967 war

BIBLIOGRAPHY

Abu Iyad with Eric Rouleau (1978) *My Home, My Land: A Narrative of the Palestinian Struggle*, New York: Times Books.

Abu-Lughod, Lila (1993/2008) *Writing Women's Worlds: Bedouin Stories*, Berkeley: University of California Press.

Abu-Sitta, Salman (2004) *Atlas of Palestine, 1948*, London: Palestine Land Society.

Al-Ali, Nadje (2007) *Iraqi Women: Untold Stories from 1948 to the Present*, London: Zed Books.

Allan, Diana (2007) 'The politics of witness: remembering and forgetting 1948 in Shatila Camp' in Ahmad H. Sa'di and Lila Abu-Lughod (eds) *Nakba: Palestine, 1948, and the Claims of Memory*, New York: Columbia University Press.

Anderson, Benedict (1983/1991) *Imagined Communities: Reflections on the Origin and Spread of Nationalism*, London: Verso.

Aruri, Naseer H. (ed.) (1989) *Occupation: Israel over Palestine*, Belmont, MA: Association of Arab-American University Graduates.

—— (2005) 'Foreword' in Nur Masalha (ed.) *Catastrophe Remembered: Palestine, Israel and the Internal Refugees*, London: Zed Books.

El-Asmar, Fouzi (1975) *To be an Arab in Israel*, London: Frances Pinter Ltd.

Berger, John (2009) 'Concerning identity' [preface] in Kamal Boullata, *Palestinian Art: From 1850 to the Present*, London: Saqi.

Bersheeth, Haim (2007) 'The continuity of trauma and struggle: recent cinematic representations of the Nakba' in Sa'di and Abu-Lughod (eds) *Nakba: Palestine, 1948, and the Claims of Memory*, New York: Columbia University Press.

Collins, John (2004) *Occupied by Memory: The Intifada Generation and the Palestinian State of Emergency*, New York: New York University Press.

Darwish, Mahmoud (1967) *Rita wa al-Bunduqiya* ['Rita and the gun'] in *Akher al-Layl* ['The End of the Night'], 2nd edn, Beirut: Dar al-'awda, pp. 45–7.

—— (1995) *Memory for Forgetfulness: Beirut, August, 1982* (trans. Ibrahim Muhawi), Berkeley: University of California Press.

Doumani, Beshara (1995) *Rediscovering Palestine: Merchants and Peasants in Jabal Nablus, 1700–1900*, Berkeley: University of California Press.

Esmier, Samera (2003) 'Law, history, memory', *Social Text* 21/2, pp. 25–48.

Fanon, Frantz (1963) *The Wretched of the Earth* (trans. Constance Farrington), New York: Grove Press.

Farsoun, Samih and Christina Zacharia (1997) *Palestine and the Palestinians*, Boulder, CO: Westview Press.

Feldman, Ilana (2008) *Governing Gaza: Bureaucracy, Authority and the Work of Rule, 1917–1967*, Durham, NC: Duke University Press.

Fraser, Ronald (1979) *Blood of Spain: An Oral History of the Spanish Civil War*, London: Allen Lane.

Gardner, David (2009) *Last Chance: The Middle East in the Balance*, London: I.B.Tauris.

Gertz, Nurith and George Khleifi (2008) *Palestinian Cinema: Landscape, Trauma and Memory*, Edinburgh: Edinburgh University Press.

Ghanem, As'ad (2001) *The Palestinian-Arab Minority in Israel, 1948–2000: A Political Study*, New York: State University of New York Press.

Halbwachs, Maurice (1980) *Collective Memory*, New York: Harper & Row.

Hammer, Juliane (2005) *Palestinians Born in Exile: Diaspora and the Search for a Homeland*, Austin: University of Texas Press.

Harlow, Barbara (1989) 'Narrative in prison: stories from the Palestinian *intifada*', *Modern Fiction Studies* 35/1, pp. 29–46.

Herzl, Theodor (1960) *The Complete Diaries of Theodor Herzl*, Volume 1, New York: Herzl Press, quoted in Ahmad H. Sa'di 'Reflections on representation, history and moral accountability' [afterword] in Sa'di and Abu-Lughod (2007) *Nakba: Palestine, 1948, and the Claims of Memory*, New York: Columbia University Press.

Hirst, David (1977/2003) *The Gun and the Olive Branch: The Roots of Violence in the Middle East*, New York: Thunder's Mouth Press.

Jayyusi, Lena (2007) 'Iterability, cumulativity, and presence: the relational figures of Palestinian memory' in Sa'di and Abu-Lughod (eds) *Nakba: Palestine, 1948, and the Claims of Memory*, New York: Columbia University Press.

Karmi, Ghada (2002) *In Search of Fatima: A Palestinian Story*, London: Verso.

Khalidi, Rashid (1997) *Palestinian Identity: The Construction of Modern National Consciousness*, New York: Columbia University Press.

—— (2006) *The Iron Cage*, Oxford: Oneworld Publications.

Khalili, Laleh (2007) *Heroes and Martyrs of Palestine: The Politics of National Commemoration*, Cambridge: Cambridge University Press.

Kimmerling, Baruch and Joel S. Migdal (1994/2003) *The Palestinian People: A History*, Cambridge, MA: Harvard University Press.

King, Nicola (2000) *Memory, Narrative, Identity: Remembering the Self*, Edinburgh: Edinburgh University Press.

Lindholm Schulz, Helena (1999) *The Reconstruction of Palestinian Nationalism: Between Revolution and Statehood*, Manchester: Manchester University Press.

Lustick, Ian (1980) *Arabs in the Jewish State: Israel's Control of a National Minority*, Austin/London: University of Texas Press.

—— (1993) *Unsettled States, Disputed Lands: Britain and Ireland, France and Algeria, Israel and the West Bank–Gaza*, Ithaca, NY, and London: Cornell University Press.

Lynd, Staughton, Sam Bahour and Alice Lynd (eds) (1994) *Homeland: Oral Histories of Palestine and Palestinians*, New York: Olive Branch Press.

Makdisi, Saree (2008) *Palestine Inside Out: An Everyday Occupation*, New York: W.W. Norton.

Makdisi, Ussama and Paul A. Silverstein (eds) (2006) *Memory and Violence in the Middle East and North Africa*, Bloomington: Indiana University Press.

Masalha, Nur (1992/2001) *Expulsion of the Palestinians: The Concept of 'Transfer' in Zionist Political Thought, 1882–1948*, Washington, DC: Institute for Palestine Studies.

—— (2000) *Imperial Israel and the Palestinians: The Politics of Expansion*, London: Pluto Press.

—— (ed.) (2005) *Catastrophe Remembered: Palestine, Israel and the Internal Refugees*, London: Zed Books.

Massad, Joseph A. (2006) *The Persistence of the Palestinian Question: Essays on Zionism and the Palestinians*, London: Routledge.

Mourad, Kenize (2003) *Our Sacred Land: Voices of the Palestine-Israeli Conflict*, Oxford: Oneworld Publications.

Muhawi, Ibrahim (1995) 'Introduction' in Mahmoud Darwish, *Memory for Forgetfulness*, Berkeley: California University Press.

Nazzal, Nafez (1978) *The Palestinian Exodus from the Galilee, 1948*, Beirut: Institute for Palestine Studies.

Nora, Pierre (1996) *Realms of Memory, Volume I: Conflicts and Divisions* (trans. Arthur Goldhammer), New York: Columbia University Press.

Pappé, Ilan (2004/2006) *A History of Modern Palestine*, Cambridge: Cambridge University Press.

—— (2006) *The Ethnic Cleansing of Palestine*, Oxford: Oneworld Publications.

Parmenter, Barbara (1994) *Giving Voices to Stones: Places and Identity in Palestinian Literature*, Austin: University of Texas Press.

Passerine, Louisa (1989) 'Women's personal narratives' in Personal Narratives Group (ed.) *Interpreting Women's Lives: Feminist Theory and Personal Narratives*, Bloomington: Indiana University Press.

Perks, Robert and Alistair Thomson (eds) (1998/2009) *The Oral History Reader*, 2nd edn, London: Routledge.

Peteet, Julie (2005) *Landscape of Hope and Despair*, Philadelphia: Pennsylvania University Press.

Popular Memory Group (1982) 'Popular memory: theory, politics, method' in Richard Johnson, Gregor McLennon, Bill Swartz and David Sutton (eds) *Making Histories*, Minneapolis: University of Minnesota Press.

Rabinowitz, Dan and Khawla Abu-Baker (2005) *Coffins on Our Shoulders: The Experience of the Palestinian Citizens of Israel*, Berkeley: University of California Press.

Rouhana, Nadim (1997) *Identities in Conflict: Palestinian Citizens in an Ethnic Jewish State*, New Haven, CT: Yale University Press.

Roy, Sara (1989) 'The Gaza Strip: critical effects of the occupation' in Naseer Aruri (ed.) *Occupation: Israel over Palestine*, Belmont, MA: Association of Arab-American University Graduates.

Sabbagh, Karl (2006) *Palestine: A Personal History*, London: Atlantic Books.

Sa'di, Ahmad (2007) 'Reflections on representation, history and moral accountability' [afterword] in Sa'di and Abu-Lughod (eds) *Nakba: Palestine, 1948, and the Claims of Memory*, New York: Columbia University Press.

Sa'di, Ahmad and Lila Abu-Lughod (eds) (2007) *Nakba: Palestine, 1948, and the Claims of Memory*, New York: Columbia University Press.

Said, Edward (1979) *The Question of Palestine*, New York: Vintage Books.

—— (1984) 'The mind of winter: reflections on life in exile' in *Harper's* (September), p. 50.

—— (1986/1993) *After the Last Sky: Palestinian Lives*, London: Vintage Books.

—— (1989) '*Intifada* and independence' in Zachary Lockman and Joel Beinin (eds) *Intifada: The Palestinian Uprising against Israeli Occupation*, Boston: South End Press, pp. 5–22.

—— (1994) 'Permission to narrate' in Said, *The Politics of Dispossession*, New York: Pantheon.

—— (1999) *Out of Place: A Memoir*, New York: Knopf.

—— (2000a) 'Invention, memory, and place' in *Critical Inquiry* 26/2 (Winter), pp. 175–92.

—— (2000b) *Reflections on Exile and Other Essays*, Cambridge, MA: Harvard University Press.

—— (2000c/2002) *The End of the Peace Process*, London: Granta Publications.

Sayigh, Rosemary (1979/2007) *The Palestinians: From Peasants to Revolutionaries*, London: Zed Books.

—— (1994) *Too Many Enemies: The Palestinian Experience in Lebanon*, London: Zed Books.

Sayigh, Yezid (1997) *Armed Struggle and the Search for State: The Palestinian National Movement, 1949–1993*, Oxford: Oxford University Press.

Shlaim, Avi (2000) *The Iron Wall: Israel and the Arab World*, London: Penguin.

—— (2007) *Lion of Jordan*, London: Allen Lane.

Slymovics, Susan (1998) *The Object of Memory: Arab and Jew Narrate the Palestinian Village*, Philadelphia: University of Pennsylvania Press.

Smith, Roger (2003) *Stories of Peoplehood: The Politics and Morals of Political Membership*, Cambridge: Cambridge University Press.

Swedenburg, Ted (2003) *Memories of Revolt: The 1936–1939 Rebellion and the Palestinian National Past*, Fayetteville: University of Arkansas Press.

Terkel, Studs (1970/1986) *Hard Times: An Oral History of the Great Depression*, New York: The New Press.

—— (1984) *The Good War: An Oral History of World War II*, New York: The New Press.

Turki, Fawaz (1988) *Soul in Exile: Lives of a Palestinian Revolutionary*, New York: Monthly Review Press.

INDEX